One Long Summer

One Long Summer

A Journey
Around the World

Mark Dalton

Matador
9 Priory Business Park,
Wistow Road, Kibworth Beauchamp,
Leicestershire. LE8 0RX
Tel: 0116 279 2299
Email: books@troubador.co.uk
Web: www.troubador.co.uk/matador
Twitter: @matadorbooks

ISBN 978 1788037 723

British Library Cataloguing in Publication Data.
A catalogue record for this book is available from the British Library.

Printed and bound by CPI Group (UK) Ltd, Croydon, CR0 4YY
Typeset in 11 pt Minion Pro by Troubador Publishing Ltd, Leicester, UK

Matador is an imprint of Troubador Publishing Ltd

To anyone whose ordinary existence leads them in search of life affirming adventure. You don't have to live vicariously, the world is waiting for you to find it for yourself.

A mind that is stretched by a new experience can never go back to its old dimensions.

— **Oliver Wendell Holmes, Sr. (1858)**

THE BACK STORY

Before starting at the beginning, there's a back story that needs telling to put this adventurous tale into perspective. I was born in 1963, and like it was for a lot of less well-off families of that era, the transport of the masses was a motorbike, old British Iron, BSA and Triumphs being the bikes of choice. To this day I don't know what make my dad's was, but it tugged a caravan-sized sidecar. That early introduction to two-wheeled transport became an enduring feature of my life. At 16 via a 50cc Yamaha FS1E I found freedom and, girls and consequently lost something as well. Life was a never-ending vastness of time stretching out before me. I grew up in the '70s but my parents didn't make it past their early sixties and so we move on.

One too much too young, one this was a bad idea and one good but short-lived marriage later; hey, three times married is rock 'n' roll, baby! I'm forty-something with a teenage daughter. Life has used up half of my time on the planet. Time to hit the reset button. Do I really want to carry on doing the same job I have always done for the rest of my life? So things change. Same company, same office, new job, new responsibilities, and new benefits. Yes, Dr BUPA, I probably do drink too much. Yes, I am a little overweight. Yes, my dad did die young. Yes, I do get the odd heart palpitation. Is that bad? There's that reset button again. I now have my own mechanical tick to accompany every heartbeat; Captain Hook would get the jitters around me! New valves do wonders for the human heart as much as the numerous engines I have worked on. My heart has been physically and, strangely, metaphorically fixed in the same procedure. I need to make use of this new life I have been given. Sat in hospital for a week, I get strange dreams and ideas.

A vague idea to visit my brother who lives in Asia develops into a plan to see more of this little blue planet. I promise my ex-father-in-law to see it through as he stopped by to visit as I recuperate. He's had chemotherapy that ultimately failed to make it all right for him. A promise is a promise; I tell everyone I know of my plans and I'm committed. Life is too short. Work agrees to me taking a year out. That bit was easy; the money might be a bit tougher. Guess I need to put the hours in; this is going to take more than a £10 lottery win.

PART ONE

DREAMS, IDEAS AND PLANS

PART ONE

'BORN FREE'

– Kid Rock

My initial idea for this twelve-month journey of exploration and discovery was born from a vague thought of visiting my brother, although the reason is a moot point now! The journey became the reason. I gave it life and it sprouted wings like a dragon that hasn't learnt to breathe fire yet. You know it's small and sweet but will eventually outgrow you and is likely to set your very soul on fire.

Oh, how I planned; oh, how I dallied with ideas, routes and places to visit. I scoured the internet for places of interest. I bought maps and I was forever scribbling notes to myself. I was always thinking about trip-related things to investigate, ideas that popped into my head as I lay awake at night or was bored with yet another technical conversation at work. Meetings at work proved particularly fruitful for ideas as my mind wandered ahead to far-flung continents and exotic jungles. I read about other people's travels. I joined internet forums where all the world's expertise is shared freely, however misguided that 'expert' might be. Some of those ideas and plans made it through to reality. Others withered on the vine with no good roots in reality and no inspirational irrigation to help them develop and grow.

Like all great ideas, this one was simple. I wanted to explore the world travelling on a motorbike. Two major milestones were an initial target; those were to stop off to visit my brother who was currently resident in Cambodia and the second to be in Melbourne for Christmas to visit a friend who had emigrated to Australia, but it is so much more than that.

Those early uneducated route plans included a route through Europe and beyond, on a road yet to be decided due to HM Government's travel advice to avoid Georgia. I looked at crossing the Black Sea as an alternative route into Russia and across the border into Kazakhstan. I always saw Kazakhstan as a challenge, but one that I relished. Over the Chinese border and passing north of the Himalayas would take me down to Vietnam, Cambodia and Thailand. After resting body and mind for a while, I planned to head south into Malaysia and on to Indonesia's multiple islands. Sea freighting the bike on to Australia, where, allowing for immigration difficulties that I had heard were sometimes tough to overcome, I planned to journey around the east coast and down to Melbourne to meet up with my friend at Christmas. From there, hopefully I could catch a container ship heading to the USA, where landing on the west coast I wanted to follow the legendary Route 66 across the states to Chicago – did someone mention that this IS the road to Amarillo?

It all sounded easy written down that quickly, but I knew from the start it would be a life-defining experience. Straight away I was completely focused on achieving my planned departure date and I knew what bike I wanted to use; a Yamaha XT660Z Ténéré is the ready-made adventure bike for the job as far as I could see. The simplicity and light weight are its advantages; with

4

no sophisticated electronics and rugged mechanicals, it would be the perfect tool.

Lots of planning to do and lots of things to sort out prior to it happening, but the seed had been planted; it just needed encouragement and careful propagation to grow into a mighty adventure.

'WAKE ME UP WHEN SEPTEMBER ENDS'

– Green Day

Let's time travel back to how I saw things as my plans
developed in 2013 and onwards.
Cue clichéd wavy lines on the cinema screen.

Summer dreaming, August 2013 – where am I in the
plan? Well, it all seems to be at a bit of a lull right now;
there is still loads to do and I need to get things moving
along. I have made progress with the bike and am now
the proud owner of a Kawasaki KLE650 Versys. It was
advertised fairly locally, so after a trip to view it, and
despite some umming and ahhing about whether I
was making the right decision, money changed hands
and I returned with plans whizzing around my head of
modifying this genial commuter bike into an 'AdVersys'
to cope with the journey. It's not the bike I originally
planned, but a few things made me change my mind, one
of the biggest being the cost of the carnet. A carnet de
passage is a temporary import document that I need to
enable me to cross some borders with a vehicle, and, due
to a very complex calculation, the cost of the document is
dependent on the value of the vehicle, so keeping the cost
down was a primary concern. I always wanted to avoid

the heavyweight BMW and KTM adventure motorcycles anyway as a light, easily manoeuvrable and nimble bike holds far more interest for me. I also don't want to appear like some rich Westerner passing through a poor country as flashing the cash just isn't my way.

A trip to the international motorcycle show at the NEC in Birmingham provided an opportunity for some bargain purchases, one being a new Shark helmet with a lift-up front section. Chosen over the usual adventure – style helmets as it provides a normal full-face helmet protection with the added bonus of being able to open up the front of the helmet to allow better communication, and, because the front goes all the way over the top and to the back of the helmet, riding with it as an open-face helmet is entirely possible. It's not the cheapest of helmets, but a few price comparisons at the show provided it at the right price on the day. An RST Pro series adventure — style textile jacket with removable lining and plenty of air vents was also purchased after a little bit of haggling over the price.

Money is still tight. My saving plans have, unsurprisingly, not gone very well over the past few months with money to spend on things I need to get sorted, but I'm still on track. Moving on!

Bonfires and fireworks, November 2013 – The year is awash with autumn leaves and as it becomes the dying embers of the raging fire that it was in July, setting off draws closer. When the New Year dawns the culmination of my plans will be in sight. It's all becoming real. Yet there is still so much to do. I am gathering the bits I need, stashing away stuff that I think I will find useful. There will come a time when I have to lay out all the kit and try to actually fit it onto or into the bike. There's a whole new challenge!

How do I plan for a year on the road? Throw away stuff that I won't need and carry the essential things I will need? What is essential and what is not? I guess I will find out! This is a voyage of self-discovery as much as a journey of exploration. I am overcoming worrying thoughts about giving up on life's little luxuries, my books and TV channels. My big, stupid, fantastic four-wheel drive pick-up truck; my guitar; my CD collection and memories in all my belongings around me. What is important I will store; what I can replace or live without will go. The most difficult possession to let go will be the Mitsubishi truck. But it will be replaced by the freedom to embark on this adventure. In the end, remembering the reasons behind my decision to set myself on this course is what's important, the once-in-a-lifetime chance to follow a dream and achieve an ambition. Everything else I can sort out later. Onwards and upwards; keeping focused on the target is what's important right now, I think, in this little pool of calm before the real organisational storm starts. After Christmas I will have to kick it all into gear and get moving again. But until then it's a case of saving what money I can, spending as little as possible and working wherever possible. Can we have another log on the fire, Mr Scrooge?

New Year, January 2014 – As I reached the year of departure, time marched on. After speaking to folks who had recently travelled across Kazakhstan, I realised I was probably allowing far too much time to travel that part of

8

the journey. I sat down with a calendar, a pen and some free time, working my way back from the Christmas deadline in Melbourne to try to work out some more settled dates. Not sure how realistic it is and I have to accept that delays, diversions and distractions will happen. Also, I might make up time in areas I don't expect, so all this is a bit 'finger in the air' guesswork. Bear with me; it's how I live my life!

At the end of April 2014 I will depart towards Holland and Germany, crossing Austria and the Alps, heading for the Stelvio Pass by the beginning of May. Entering Italy, I will spend approximately three weeks travelling around taking in the Italian rounds of the World Superbike and MotoGP series, before aiming to arrive at Brindisi on the south-east coast for the last weekend in May to take a ferry to Greece. I intend to spend two weeks exploring Greece before entering Turkey around the third week of June. I reckon a week along the Black Sea coast will see me in Georgia by the end of June and across the Caucasus Mountains into Russia by the following week. Two weeks should be enough to travel up to Volgograd and back down to the Kazakhstani border by mid-July, just in time to be welcomed by the blast of summer heat! Allowing a week to ten days to get to Taraz on the Kyrgyzstani border by the end of July leaves me five days to cross Kyrgyzstan to get to the Chinese border by the beginning of August. Now here's a tough one: I've read it will take five days to get to Kashgar and across the Karakorum highway to get to Pakistan, then two weeks to get to Nepal and into Kathmandu. Aiming to airfreight to Bangkok by the last weekend of August, to travel on to Ho Chi Minh City

9

to meet my brother a week to ten days later around the last week of September. Depart Ho Chi Minh City by the middle of September and travel back through Cambodia and Thailand to reach Malaysia by the end of October, taking in the Sepang MotoGP round. Then ship to Perth, Australia, by the beginning of December, giving me three weeks to travel across the Nullarbor Plain and the Great Ocean Road to Melbourne by Christmas. From there the plans are sketchy(er), but getting across the Pacific Ocean to the USA will require some thinking. Crossing that continent should be achievable, and getting across the Atlantic Ocean should be easy after my experiences getting that far.

Slipping time, February 2014 – With three and a bit months to go, I have made another change to the route I had planned. After taking a long look at what I want to achieve, the costs and time involved in travelling through Russia, Kazakhstan, Kyrgyzstan and China are a big overhead to the overall plan. It feels like a bit of a compromise, but after getting in touch with some other overland travellers who are planning similar adventures, a route across Iran seems a viable alternative. There appear to be some security issues in Pakistan, but then there are even bigger ones in northern Pakistan, where the Himalayan crossing ends, so either way there are risks involved, but then if I was worried about that I would stay at home!

Financial and time savings will help me push on to the rest of the adventure, and the challenge of India will make up for the loss of crossing the Himalayas. My doctor had already recommended I stay away from that 5km-high route, so for once I guess I will listen to advice. Moving on, having made that (difficult) decision, I can put plans into action and start making them happen.

The bike is almost completely equipped. I've fitted a high front mudguard to provide some extra clearance over rough terrain. After a few failed experimental mudguards, I found the front mudguard from a KTM 990 Supermoto is a perfect fit. I have a pair of bargain eBay LED spotlights fitted, hand guards, a compass and an adjustable screen. Another eBay bargain, a pair of metal panniers made by a German company called Dar Box, and my best purchase of all, the pannier rack to fit them to the bike. The last item was purchased online from the USA after a fruitless online search around the UK and Europe failed to provide any affordable alternatives. However, after ordering, it failed to arrive and I was refunded the full cost. The supplier also claimed back the cost from the shipper for the lost item. Everyone's a winner. Except two weeks later the postman delivered a package from America. Sometimes you just have to keep your mouth shut!

I still have a few maintenance tasks to undertake. My own kit is sorted. Paperwork still needs fully sorting out and the money needs gathering together from the disparate sources across which I have spread it.

It has also been a month of ups and downs. Problems with the route plan due to upheaval in Pakistan and reports of border crossing difficulties. The small matter of an overland bicycle rider only just escaping with his life after a hand grenade attack has meant a lack of enthusiasm for travelling in that region. My own timescales not matching up with fellow travellers' plans, in the end I have decided that I need to refocus on my original plan, which has been for some time to plough my own furrow and chase my own dreams. Trying to make my plans fit in with someone else's isn't how it should be; if our plans coincide, then all well and good. As much as it would be good to travel with a like-minded group of folks, that was not the original plan, and I have been diverted from the purity of that initial thought because I have sought comfort in companionship and a sharing of the difficulties instead of looking after myself and my own thoughts.

Yes, I will find times when it would indeed be very nice to have someone to lean on, someone to go to for guidance or even encouragement. But finding my own way, reaching into my own thoughts and psyche' will be character-building and cleansing for the soul. Is that too much of a cliché, I wonder? Will I just want to run away from the difficult bits? It's a possibility. Of course I am fully expecting to find fellow travellers en route. I like the idea of chance and luck coming into whom I meet along the road. Finding my own limits is part of the adventure, I think.

Time to get moving! Still lots to do and time is marching on. While my plans will mostly chase the sun around our blue planet during the northern and southern hemisphere summers, the winter in the UK seems to be doing its best to make sure I appreciate a bit of warm sunshine. Time will tell.

'The best laid schemes O' Mice an' Men,
Gang aft agley,
An' lea'e us nought but grief an' pain,
For promis'd joy'

– Robert Burns, TO A MOUSE

March 2014 – All my plans are suddenly in tatters. A couple of weeks ago I had an emergency operation to repair a torn retina in my left eye. My planned departure for the end of April is not going to happen. The doctor has told me to look (ha!) at a recovery of three to six months. It is also expected that I will develop a cataract that will require further surgery to repair. Not going ahead with my original plan is a major knockback after three years of planning to get to this stage. The best option for me now is to get everything resolved with my eyesight and allow time for it to settle down. On top of that, I have to make sure that I give my employer the notice they need to cover my sabbatical. Plans that have already been put in place now have to be readjusted. Difficult, to say the least. After being forced to sit still during the initial recovery, I had a long time to ponder the failure to launch. I have to admit that even with not being able to see, I was in a dark place for a while.

One month later it's still hard to accept the delay easily. An appointment at the hospital 'saw' two of the three stitches removed from my eye in a brief tear-inducing painful moment! The third will remain and hopefully dissolve of its own accord, all of which has removed some of the irritation I had been experiencing. The doctor identified the beginnings of a cataract and I will have to revisit at the end of June to pick up the next phase of the recovery. The doctor was also concerned about something in my right eye, which will be checked at the same time. Happy days!

Enough of the health issues! This is a story about travelling, and having accepted that I will be delayed for twelve months, I have to be positive and re-target a new departure date, which I plan to do at the same time next year. Id Est. The last weekend in April 2015. In the meantime, I will utilise the twelve months to save more money, which might allow for a few luxuries like hotels along the way. It also gives me time to do some other preventative maintenance to the bike that I had not scheduled for. So, taking the positives from the whole affair, I will be better prepared than I originally intended. Keeping that positive line of thought has been difficult, but, given no option, it's the only way I can proceed. Twelve months' delay to the experience of a lifetime is a small price to pay. One other positive is the news that I will become a grandad in September and consequently will be at home to see that occasion. Feeling old!

One week post-planned departure and sat at work thinking about where I should be is difficult to deal with, but it is what it is. My eye is actually not too bad at the moment. The irritation dropped off after the stitches were removed. Next for the recovery is a check-up at the end of June to look at a cataract op. Fun! Fun! Fun!

On the plus side I have been doing improvements

to the bike that I had not originally thought I would do. So far, I have upgraded the forks with new progressive springs and new oil. I have ordered a custom-built rear shock to cope with the increase in my weight and the kit over the standard set-up, and a test ride will prove it to be a worthwhile investment. On the weekend I had originally planned to depart, I still packed a bag and set off on a little jaunt. It was just a shame I had to come back home the next day. Later in the year I'll have a mini adventure on the bike to somewhere warm and sunny, hopefully. In the meantime, let's jump forward in time to catch up a little.

July 2014 – After a bit of a break from planning and thinking too much, settling into the daily schedule and generally working all the time! It feels like I should start getting things moving again as the year races by and it's already August. I would have been on the road for more than three months by now. Conversely, it's only eight months until I set off on my journey. This is a strange place to be, neither here nor there.

I have had a couple of mini adventures, first taking a trip down to Brittany on my Triumph motorcycle in June. I managed to carry a surprising amount of camping gear on the back seat and had a thoroughly enjoyable week in the warm French sunshine. Lots of glorious French food and wine, warm nights, hot days and buckets of local mussels made it a trip to remember. A month later and the adventure-prepared Kawasaki was fully loaded for a trip to Cornwall and the chance to test out some of my collected camping paraphernalia. A tarpaulin extension on the front of the tent proved itself to be an invaluable addition and I slept extremely well on a lightweight inflatable mattress. Apart from the bike's drive chain leaping off the sprockets about ten miles from home, it went very well. I knew the chain was worn, with a severe tight spot. I had hoped to make it last a while and replace it during the winter, but it cried enough and after slipping it back into place, we limped home without further mishap. One thing I did find out was that the seat on the Versys was not at all comfortable for any type of long distance. Since getting back, it has been suitability modified with the addition of a gel insert and a new cover. A sheepskin on top of that will, I hope, improve the comfort situation even further. It remains to be seen if it is viable for more than a couple of hours' non-stop travel.

One other short trip I did in June was to go to the 'Horizons Unlimited' website's HUBB meeting at Donington Park, which proved a very enjoyable and inspiring weekend with lots of great travel stories, adventure films, and some useful advice. A mix of vehicles, some well travelled and others seemingly kitted up for an adventure but mostly unused.

Since then it's been a case of all work and no play. Earning cash, stashing savings and sometimes spending more than I should! But right now it feels that having been given the additional time to save I don't have to try so hard. Maybe that's a bad thing, but sometimes life is for living and three months ago I was about to manage on what I had. If I can't manage better on what I will have, it was a fool's plan from the start. I am seriously considering a ride to the Adriatic coast in September, from Wednesday to Thursday the following week, taking in the MotoGP round at Misano. Part of me is saying do it, another part is saying spend the money on a few bits I need to do around the house. Troubled times! Hardly!

On the house subject, I am now leaning more and more towards selling up. What I will do when I get back I don't know, but I have lived here for ten years, longer than I have ever lived anywhere in my life, and it feels like time to move on, yet it is somehow difficult to imagine doing so. I guess that's the downside to settling in somewhere, you get to know people and places get familiar. There are positive and negatives to every situation in life. I have been thrilled at the uncertainty of travel on my little trips. Not knowing where I will stay on that night, getting lost and finding my way with equal aplomb. It feels like what I should be doing. I have gained another insight into what works for me. So the plan for now and in the New Year is to start the build-up to departure again.

One major milestone before all that will be the birth of my first grandchild in a few short weeks from now. An occasion I wasn't going to be around to see had initial plans come to fruition. More to follow on that one!

Grandad will report in again soon! In the meantime, I'm buying kit and gathering stuff together.

December 2014 – So, after the health issues with my sight last year that delayed my departure, I have reset my plans, which in the end has been something of a blessing as it allowed me to be slightly better prepared and more confident in my plans and route. Due to recent world events, I will stay away from Middle Eastern routes and head north. So the final definite and totally cast-in-stone plan includes Azerbaijan and crossing the Caspian Sea to Kazakhstan then across Siberia to Vladivostok and a ship to South Korea before shipping the bike directly to Australia, travelling down the east coast of Australia, despite advice that December isn't the best time to be in the Northern Territory, before returning to my original idea of heading to New Zealand. My brother is moving to South Korea so I will spend a little time mooching around there while I sort out shipping the bike directly to Australia. There are lots of shipping agency websites that seem to suggest that it is entirely feasible. It frees me up for a little bit of R&R off the bike to travel through the South China Sea and Pacific islands before getting myself to Australia.

The bike is prepped, apart from fitting a set of new tyres before I depart. I have all the kit I need and probably more, but that will sort itself out as I travel. The money situation is good and I don't envisage many issues. I have still got to sort out renting the house out for twelve months. I will look at that early January 2015. Hopefully, it shouldn't be too difficult. The carnet should be a little bit cheaper by missing out Indonesia. It's a very complicated calculation, but there is a refundable deposit meaning the total cost will be acceptable.

I hope to be able to arrange most visas en route so that I'm not stuck being at certain borders by certain dates, but will look more into that over the next couple of weeks. I would definitely like to sort out the visas for as far as Russia as that shouldn't be too difficult, I hope. A quick glance at the prices quoted by TheVisaMachine.com gave me an idea of the costs and benefits of using a visa agent to sort out the paperwork.

'TIME'

– Pink Floyd

January 2015 – I have lots more to say before a lifetime slips by. It's a relative thing, I know, but the years are definitely shorter to me than they used to be. I passed another birthday and my grandson (Noah) was born. It's like standing on the pavement staring at the TV sets in the shop window without being in there. I want to be the swashbuckling adventurous star of my own series; I want to get going before the series ends. I don't know how many episodes there are, but each one is another step along the way.

Back to my planning, the carnet application is going in the post this week. After further investigations, I only need it for Australia. I will value the bike at the minimum accepted value of £1000 on the application. The actual true value to me is far greater, but I will see what happens. I have the paperwork for the visa applications and I will get those moving in the next week as well. I am going to get the Azerbaijani, Kazakhstani and Russian visas before travelling, which does to a certain extent tie me down to a couple of fairly specific dates, but that can't be helped. One issue is that I now have to provide biometrics for the Russian application, which will require a personal visit to the application office in London. I will find passage on a freight ship from Baku in Azerbaijan to Aktau in

Kazakhstan across the Caspian Sea, and, as the first European Games will happen in Baku just before I arrive, I wonder if the infamous ex-Soviet shipping will be one of the many improvements going on in that developing country. Things are moving and the clock is ticking.

Tick-tock.

'TRAVELLIN' MAN'
– Bob Seger

February 2015 – Plans coming together. Visa applications are in! So I have no passport at the moment. Won't get far then! I need that back with the required visa stamps inserted. Time, tide and Russian visa applications wait for no man, it seems. I'm delaying paying for the carnet as the RAC date it from the date it is posted from their office, so at the end of March I'll pay up and wait for delivery. What's left? The list is getting shorter. I've still got to service the bike, but that's a job that I can do in a day: a warmer day! It's still icy cold up here in the Peak District. I've still got a few house re-decorations to finish, but then I've always had a few house re-decorations to do in the ten years I have lived in it. It has always 'done the job' for me; I have other more interesting things to do or buy than silk finish paint and wallpaper or new carpets. It's been warm(ish), I have my music, a comfy bed to sleep in, somewhere to fix the bikes and park the car off-road; what more do I need? Except now it has to be more respectable, because no one wants to live in the mess I would leave behind. Not that I dislike decorating; it's quite a satisfying task when it's all done.

With the road beckoning, I have booked a B&B on the south coast for the initial part of the journey; it's getting close. Everyone I see asks me how long to go, but I'm not counting the days as it all went wrong last year, even though an eye check-up confirmed it's all good. No issues expected over the next few years. The doctor advised me to expect a cataract following the eye surgery last year, but it's not developed and not expected to until I get older. Older than I am, that is!

In the meantime, I've been having a life clear-out. I have been amazed at how much 'stuff' I have gathered over the last ten years in this house. I've never been a hoarder, but then I've never lived in one place for this long, so perhaps haven't had the same opportunity to not throw stuff away. Well, now I have. The local charity shops have benefitted from a few donations. Do I really need a dog-eared 2005 British Grand Prix programme? Nope, guess not; but it was nice to read through it before it went in the recycling! Time to sit back and let it happen. No point stressing; other people can do that for me, moving on.

March 2015 – Russian visa sorted! A day trip to London to complete a brief twenty-minute visa application process was simple. It also gave me a chance to run the bike down the M1 and back on a mildly chilly day at 6°C. There is no such thing as bad weather, just the wrong clothes. Fortunately, I am well equipped and with the benefit of heated grips it was a less chilly breeze. I got in and out of Olde Londinium with no issues at all. So while I wait for the postman to deliver the passport with all the required stamps in place, I have time to sort out some bike servicing. One thing I discovered on returning home from London was that one of the new brake lines I installed had been rubbing against the front wheel, which rather fortunately only failed just as I pulled onto the drive at home. Oops! Oh well, better there than earlier or later!

So what's left to do? Spending more money, it seems! I signed up for a house rental management with a local agent. Putting that in place increases costs but it does give me peace of mind. Basically, I can go on my travels and not worry about sorting out any rental issues. Renting my house comes with several expenses that I could do without. Landlord insurance, energy performance certificates, gas safety certificates and the wonderful fee payable to the mortgage company for them to say yes I can rent it, which comes in at more than one month's mortgage payment! Using my best txt abbreviation, WTF! All that aside, I'm in a pretty good place and want to just settle my mind to the actual fact of leaving and changing my life for the next twelve months. With a mix of excitement and trepidation, I need to find a comfort zone to deal with the last few weeks leading up to departure.

April 2015 – Showery April heralds the arrival of spring and I can look at the departure in days rather than months or weeks. Although most preparations are either done or are on plan, I keep getting rushes of nervous sensations. There is a sense of just wanting to get going. I think it will get more intense as the date gets nearer; I suppose those are natural feelings. I would be strange if I felt completely casual about it, but nevertheless it is slightly unnerving. This is the last chance saloon before I hit the road. Metaphorically speaking, I hope! (Note to self not to use that phrase again!) So, rather than bore anyone reading this with housekeeping tasks I still need to finish off, all I'm going to say is that I hope this adventure is something you will enjoy reading about. I hope I have the vocabulary to communicate my experiences and thoughts as I travel our little blue planet. I hope I can illustrate that not everything you read in the papers or hear on the news is true about people and places outside your home. I hope my belief is right! If it's not, I might be in for a tough time! Not that I'm going into this totally innocent of the wider world.

I have plans to keep any interested followers up to date with a blog, YouTube videos and Flickr pictures whenever and wherever an internet connection is available to me. I would hate to think I might be talking to myself! I guess that's something else I will have to get used to!

PART TWO

THE ADVENTURE

Time to get moving!

1 DEPARTURE – LE GRAND DEPART

Clearing the house of useless bric-a-brac had been difficult. Parking my Triumph motorbike at a temporary home was thought-provoking, and selling my Mitsubishi truck was a real tearjerker. The day arrived, and with it came mixed feelings of stress and confusion. Everything was a blur as I packed the last few things onto the bike that I hadn't done the night before. So much for travelling on a lightweight bike! With the help of a few friends, the final moments at home were a scene of chaotic disorganisation. In the end I just left, sure that I hadn't done everything I needed to, but realising it was too late to worry about it. The bike felt cumbersome and overladen with far too much stuff. Quite how I would manage to travel the distances I was going to was mind-boggling!

My final preparation for leaving England was an easy ride south, blessed with crisp spring weather, to an overnight stop in Folkestone. Leaving the Eurotunnel departure gate the following morning and heading for the carriage that would transport me under the English Channel was emotional. The previous day and the actual leaving had felt like an ending rather than a beginning. It tore at my heart. Everything that I had hidden away in my mind, the feelings of trepidation, all my inner fears came out like the breaking of a dam wall that let a flood of tears blur my last sight of England, where the language and customs are so natural and familiar. After wiping my eyes and straightening myself up on the Channel transit, I got talking to a group of Welsh bike riders who were heading for a week around France and Germany. During this conversation, I had the first taste of explaining my journey, something that I would repeat hundreds of times over the coming months.

2 FRANCE – IL PLEUT DES CORDES

Arriving in France on a Sunday means the whole country is mostly fermé! The thunderous clouds overhead as I left Calais matched my mood. Like a newborn, I felt lost and not able to cope with what I had taken on. I had read lots about travellers being excited about the journey, but my initial feelings were quite the opposite. Instead of thrills and excitement, I felt downbeat and emotional. Downbeat is probably too strong a description, but not on the high I had expected. The highs will come, I'm sure; I just started at the wrong bit! Right or wrong, this is the beginning. That in itself is a step in the right direction as all week clearing the house has felt like an ending.

After being ejected from the Channel Tunnel onto French soil, the road south-east was sodden. Heavyweight, oppressive, rolling grey-blue clouds filled the sky to the edge of the world, where sky and land met in a haze of falling rain. I need to step beyond that immediate horizon. It's funny how after all the planning, the thinking, the anticipation, all the excitement, years and months of working towards taking the first step, it has been tougher than I ever imagined it might be. But, despite all that, I have to renew my optimism for this adventure. With a little luck, the initial down will be followed by huge highs and there is plenty to look forward to over the coming weeks and months.

My first attempt at an overnight stop was thwarted when I looked for a campsite. I followed the signs from the main road to find it closed. A quick question to a local gent walking his dog advised it was "fermé jusqu'à ce que le premier mai." Sat in a travel hotel just outside Reims listening to constant heavy rain, it might have been a blessing. Tomorrow may see me at the German border and country number two, unless the rain curtails my enthusiasm for mile munching. Nice weather for frogs! Moving on!

Day two and I've only travelled about 150km in biblical rain so bad I couldn't see the road through the spray. I cried enough at Nancy and pulled into a service area to warm up with a mug of coffee while I used the free Wi-Fi to book the nearest Ibis hotel and called it a day. With wet bike gear gently steaming as it dried out, hung above the room heaters turned up to maximum, I contemplated the lack of any celebratory reasons for popping corks while I travelled through Champagne country. I haven't seen the sun yet! I'm sure there will come a time when I pray for rain, but can someone please organise a little more of an even spread across the trip? All of it in one day is a bit much, thanks.

Despite the torrential rain, my state of mind is a little clearer today. I haven't had the chance to chill out with a tent and campfire to get my head around being out here. It's just been a pack/travel/unpack routine so far, which is not what I wanted. I had hoped to ease my mind into the process of travelling, the different routine and timescales. I will find that sweet spot; it is there waiting. The testing weather hasn't helped either, not much fun to be found yet. But I knew this was more than just some simple holiday. I have to rearrange my thoughts and grasp what I am doing out here with no one but me and nowhere to stay each night until I find it. It's what I do quite well, just more of it.

I need that sunshine to help with the process. I would have liked to enjoy the scenery and appreciate the countryside I'm passing through, but I didn't see much of it today. Whatever the climate throws at me tomorrow I will be out of France, heading upwards towards the mountains.

While writing what was to become a ritual of writing my daily diary, my iPod, set on shuffle, played Led Zeppelin, 'WHEN THE LEVEE BREAKS'. Apt! Moving on!

3 SWITZERLAND – ALPINE PASSES

After being rudely woken by the cleaner knocking on the door at 8.15, I was on the road early. Brighter skies accompanied me at last out of Nancy on a wonderfully entertaining ride to Mulhouse, where dark clouds gathered again, threatening to spoil my fun. Skirting around the industrial greyness of Chimnes, I followed the road towards Basel, and after crossing the Swiss border I stopped for a lunch break and fuel at a service station. My lack of language skills was immediately apparent as Swiss German confused me even more than my meagre French had. After picking up an expensive paper map on my way out, I headed towards Zurich, where I passed the first UK-registered vehicle I had seen since leaving Calais. Preferring to take the scenic route over mountains and past lakes, I ignored signs directing me to Zurich city centre as the road's altitude climbed. When heavy rain returned under leaden skies, I stopped at a fuel station and took the opportunity to put on my one-piece waterproofs again, while chatting to a retired English couple in their camper van heading south for some early summer sunshine. A few minutes later the road delved into a dark 2.5km tunnel that obviously led me into a parallel world where the warm sun blessed the tarmac and eased my progress. Deciding I had covered enough distance for the day, I started investigating accommodation opportunities. The picturesque lakeside town of Waldenstadt offered possibilities but at €190 for a room I passed by and found a cheaper Ibis hotel in Chur, an interesting little town that sits on the banks of the Rhine and is reputedly the oldest town in Switzerland! A few local campsites were all closed this early in the season, which is no big problem given that I'm not sure my camping equipment is up to the chilled overnight temperatures and forecast of snow. An underground car park provided shelter for my little motorbike and the chance to give it a quick check-over. My choice of tyres on the bike this far has been perfect, confidence-inspiring on wet, cold tarmac and providing grip when I needed it. I'm sure that confidence will continue under warmer climes over the border in Italy tomorrow. With everything in order, I retired for a comfortable night after being on the end of a telling-off from the owner of a Porsche 911 for having the temerity to park what he considered too close to his precious prestige motor! Bless!

An evening stroll into the town showed how considerate Swiss drivers are. Merely pausing next to a pedestrian crossing brought the traffic to a standstill. That politeness continued as I departed in the morning, albeit later than intended, at 10am as I got caught up in trying to pack up the bike a little better and failing. It did, however, give the sun chance to provide a weak attempt to warm the north-western slopes of the Alps as the road rose into the hills under a fresh pale blue sky. With light traffic and the occasional truck heavily loaded with lumber, progress to higher altitudes was good, the temperature dropping in equal measure to the rising height of the road. Near the jet-set resort of St Moritz, I stopped and added a couple of layers of my unbranded clothing, to hold off the near zero degrees cold, before summiting the mountains as the road passed the peak at Diavolezza, which translates as 'She-Devil'. The geological car crash of the European and African tectonic plates pushing the Alps ever upwards, where the windswept and snow-lined road provides plenty of lingering icy bite and illustrates to this lonely traveller how difficult the mountains must be in winter.

4 ITALY – BENVENUTO

On the southern side of the mountains the road's long sweeping curves headed down to the lower slopes and higher temperatures until at the deserted Italian border crossing, the temperature suddenly rose to twenty degrees centigrade. Like switching on a massive heater, winter was suddenly left in the mountains and spring was in full bloom. Lush greenery, gardeners tending their early spring blooms, dry roads and the approaching sound of a loud motorbike saw me giving way to an enthusiastic rider on a Yamaha R1, who was obviously revelling in the warm sunshine and dry tarmac.

I stopped at a roadside spot to admire the lower Alpine foothills and take a light lunch from my supplies. After checking my route on the map, the mountain road met a valley road through Edolo. As the road levelled out along the valley floor I missed a turn-off I was hoping to find that cut across country, and ended up following the main road towards Brescia, which included long kilometres of hot fume-filled tunnels as the road cut through the hills alongside Lago D'Isea. Despite its lack of breathable atmosphere in the tunnels, the road is apparently significantly safer than the old road along the north shore where according to local stories entire families were swallowed up in the murky waters alongside it. Eventually, after skirting around Brescia, I passed through

Salo, which was the capital of Mussolini's Italian Social Republic between 1943 and 1945. Riding along the shore of Lake Garda, I found my first campsite of the trip, where three nights cost the same as a single night in a hotel with the additional pleasure of sleeping 'under canvas' listening to the lapping waters of the lake and birds roosting in the olive trees.

Lago Di Garda – After the travelling and the rush through France I breezed through the day in Italian style. My first day of not covering any distance, zero kilometres, a day off sitting by Lago de Garda after getting up later than I have recently. No rush to leave a hotel room, sat by the lake with a simple breakfast of peppermint tea and a jar of Nutella easing me into the day. My only journey was a short trip to the local supermarket for provisions. Wine, cheese, tomatoes and olives; a man needs nothing more. Well, apart from a motorbike. The Alps crossing was amazing, but arriving in Italy eased my mind. It has always been a place I feel at peace in, I don't know why. Maybe I just get the way of life here, the passion for living without the British obsession for more than we have. I have a few weeks in Italy to find myself and relax, laugh out loud at the driving experience and marvel at the scenery. I have a week before going to Imola for the World Superbike race meeting and then a couple of weeks before the big one: the Italian round of the MotoGP world championship at Mugello.

As my equipment settles down and finds its own place, a few issues are showing up. My compass attached to the handlebars is useless as it is affected by the magnets in my tank bag. The bracket it sat on broke yesterday, but the comedy value was too valuable to abandon it, so it found a new home where I could still watch it spin round, forever pointing me in all magnetic directions. My airbed failed overnight; this early in the trip that is disappointing. I will attempt a repair from a pannier lining bag that has also split, once I get a chance. Until then, I guess I will get used to sleeping on the ground.

After three days lakeside in Garda, it was time to move on as the rain made a valiant attempt to catch up with me. It was perhaps not the best campsite in the area, I'm sure, but it gave me time to catch my breath after racing the weather since leaving the UK. While the last few days had been peaceful, the approaching weekend brought the arrival of an Italian family to their permanent caravan, moored lakeside. Their loud chatter shattering the quiet calm, but redemption was at hand with the offer of an espresso and a conversation in broken English and my limited Italian about MotoGP superstar and Italian legend Valentino Rossi.

The morning departure took me a while as everything just wouldn't happen. I got a bit hot 'n' bothered kitted up in bike gear in 24°C degree heat. I left the phone charging lead in a pannier, which meant unpacking again as I needed it for the Google Maps navigation, almost dropping the bike in the process and starting the day's journey in a fluster.

A fairly uninteresting ride across the flatlands of northern Italy's Po Plain, passing by a few strange concrete skeletal structures with For Sale signs attached, brought me to Modena, where an elderly couple meandered along a twisty road in their inevitable convertible red supercar.

I got slightly lost around the periphery of Bologna, which wouldn't be the last time on this trip. Looking for a lunchtime rest, I failed to find a shady spot that wasn't inhabited by a prostitute, not the definition of shady I was looking for! I ended up under the canopy of a closed fuel station: very picturesque! By early afternoon I was in a more entertaining and typically Italian landscape. Wonderful scenery surrounded me with the constant call of a distant cuckoo to accompany my pasta tea at a wooded hillside campsite. My next target is the world superbike round at Imola, which is about an hour's ride away. So I think this is a place to sit back for a while and enjoy the peace and tranquillity of Italy's rolling hills; the journey just got chilled out.

In complete contrast to last Monday, I'm not moving today. The sun is shining, the sky is blue, cuckoo in the distance and I'm relaxing for the day. No point rushing around this week. I've got plenty of time to explore Italy's wonderful interests, but for now it's a very pleasant twenty-four degrees with a nice, cool breeze. Why do anything else? After a long, grey, dull British winter, the first chance to sit in the sunshine is something I'm enjoying.

I have done one thing today and that was to check the bike's cooling system. I replaced the coolant with fresh mixture just before I left, but on Saturday, while riding in warm temperatures, it was making bubbling noises for a while after I switched the engine off. It's just a bit of an airlock in the system, I think. Sadly, to get at everything on the Versys you have to dismantle most of the bodywork. Even the coolant expansion tank cap is inaccessible without getting the spanners out. Nice design, Kawasaki-san! Anyway, after a bit of fiddling it's sorted, I think. Moving on!

Another peaceful night after another bottle of wine; I think I might have a night off the alcohol tonight and check my INR tomorrow. Not that it makes much difference; it seems better when I do drink. That's my excuse anyway. It was a little low last week, so I have been compensating with increased doses of Warfarin. I don't expect it to be far out when I do check. I think I'm starting to get myself a bit more organised with camping and loading the gear on the bike. I was frustrated last week by misplacing everything. In such a small space it shouldn't be possible. For anyone that has ever seen my garage, you will understand. I've always had a mischievous fairy that follows me around moving things I need and putting them back when I'm no longer looking for them. She/it seems to be accompanying me on the trip! After mentally struggling under France's overcast skies, it's amazing how a little sun and warm temperatures can ease your mind. I'm sure there are fiercer temperatures to be experienced over the coming months, but, for this sun-starved Englishman, right now it's just perfect, thanks. Looking at the map, I think Imola is about an hour and a half away. Setting off on Friday morning will see me there by around lunchtime easily. A weekend's bike racing action will be in stark contrast to the relaxing atmosphere of this Italian hillside, but that's a good thing. Contrast is what makes life interesting. Ying and yang! Not moving on! (Yet.)

On Wednesday I took an excursion to Lucca and it was a lovely day out. To get there I stayed off the main pay autoroute that goes via Firenze and took the SS64 via Porettana that runs from Bologna to Pistoia. What a fantastic road it is as it winds its way across the hills and valleys that separate this area from the west coast. As described on away.com… this quiet 85-mile (138 km) back road through the Apennine Mountains is positively bucolic. Linking Tuscany and Emilia-Romagna, it leads north-west from Pistoia, just east of Florence, to Ferrara via Bologna. It crosses thick chestnut forests, the ancient spa resort of Porretta, Terme, and small, sleepy towns. I had planned to get to Pisa for a gratuitous tower shot, but the weather looked a little inclement near the coast, and after getting lost on the autoroute around Pisa I decided to cut and run. There will be another opportunity, I'm sure. The historic town of Lucca is living testimony to ancient history, with well-preserved medieval architecture evident from every corner of its narrow winding streets. A tasty quattro formaggi pizza for lunch in the Piazza dell'Anfiteatro, which follows the elliptical shape of the former Roman amphitheatre, followed by a bottle of merlot when I got back to the campsite topped off a great day. So much for reducing my alcohol intake.

Thursday is without doubt the hottest day of the trip so far, despite the weather report predicting rain! Time to stay in the shade a bit while I sort out everything and repack; I will find the ideal balanced way of doing things. Living in and out of a few bags and panniers that I carry gets a bit difficult without some sense of organisation, which I am rubbish at, always have been; I guess it's time I learnt. I also looked up the camping availability for Imola and that seems to be okay. From what I can see on the internet there is camping available around the periphery of the park that contains the race circuit. I will leave as soon as I am ready on Friday morning and should be there for early afternoon. Well, that was the plan anyway!

Imola World Superbike weekend – After getting lost for the second time on this trip around Bologna, I arrived and set up in a very small campsite just outside town, the peaceful ambience of last week shattered by the proximity of fellow campers. The expected camping availability was absent as the local authorities had taped off the grassy banks of the Santerno river to prevent camping in the area. The town is marinated in motorsport history; the Autodromo Enzo e Dino Ferrari has been in existence since the 1950s, set in the Acque Minerali Park. It saw the classic era of Formula One and motorcycle racing. It has also witnessed its share of glory and infamous tragedy.

Some of the following is a bit of a compilation of (some alcohol-induced) thoughts over the weekend, so you'll forgive my slightly meandering line of thought:

Travelling is a funny thing. Take everything that makes your life comfortable and give it up. Leave everyone you care about and throw your lot in with strangers who don't even speak the same language. Take the simple fact of knowing where you will sleep tonight and make it an unknown. You can plan ahead a little and carry some provisions and maybe book some accommodation in advance, but in the end all of life's securities are up for discussion and suddenly the life you know and rely on is not necessarily the actual outcome. That in itself is an exciting concept but one that needs a bit of thinking about. I guess, in history, human life has not been at the comfort level that we take for granted in the modern world. Hunting for your evening meal must have had its unknowns and potentially hungry nights. In some ways, rediscovering the basic needs for living is a part of this venture. I miss satellite TV, my truck parked on the driveway with enough fuel to drive anywhere I want to, beer in the fridge, and the internet to discover yet more facts I didn't need to know or care about regarding someone's latest breakfast/night out or boredom level. So long, Facebook! I didn't need you before, I'm even more certain I don't need you now! Extracting myself from the modern world had been something of a wrench. And yet I'm still able to get online to communicate with anyone via text, phone, mail, Twitter or blog. In so many ways I am actually still connected. It's just not immediately available on demand all the time.

On holidays you still know that you will have a bed for the night and a meal at some point. My holidays over the years have to some extent followed a similar way of living to what I am doing now, but dealing with that for two weeks is part of the joy I get from living without too much of a plan. This journey feels different because it seems right now to have no end, and dealing with that is a wider experience than I have dealt with so far in my life.

I have wondered what historic explorers must have experienced without modern communications, completely cut off from their own world. While I am no Dr Livingstone deep in the African bush, I am on my own voyage of discovery. My normal life of work, nights out, a beer in the pub, getting paid monthly and all the modern trappings have been changed.

One thing about Italy that has struck me on my travels around this glorious country is how much road building has taken place to allow easy movement by motorised vehicles through what is quite challenging geography. Bridges that span whole valleys between tunnels drilled through hills and mountains that must once have cut off whole communities. Some of the older tunnels, I guess, must date from the '50s or perhaps earlier, and as such they are mostly oxygen-free zones in places. Newer ones are much nicer to ride through with built-in ventilation. There doesn't seem to have been much thought for the natural environment with some of the concrete monstrosities that divert traffic around the smaller towns deep in the valleys and often bisect the buildings from one side in the shade to the other sunlit side. It's a strange contrast of modern needs conflicting with old ways of life.

Imola world superbike weekend has been a somewhat strange affair compared to my previous experience of motorcycle race meetings. Considering the current top four most successful riders in the series are British, I have yet to actually meet any British motorcycle riders that have made the journey. My last time at an Italian round in Monza in 2002 was a sharp contrast, with a lot of Brits around. Maybe it's the case that most British bikers have got old these days and have flown to comfortable hotels! Assuming they are here at all. Maybe years of restrictive legislation and nanny overprotective parenting have prevented a new generation from enjoying the freedom and thrill of two-wheeled transport that is the accepted norm in the rest of Europe. That is a sad thought for a generation that didn't discover the same freedom of my own teenage experience.

As I sit here on a balmy Saturday evening with a (plastic) glass of red wine, the rumble of motorcycle engines and the smell of BBQ smoke hanging in the air along with the expectation of a great day's racing ahead tomorrow, life seems pretty cool. There's a couple of things missing that would make it complete, but for right now I don't need much else to make me happy. I struggle with the monotony of normal day-to-day life at times, always have. Working to earn a living, living in a world where money means happiness to most people. It's true that money makes life easier and, let's be honest, without money I wouldn't have been able to make this adventure happen, but living life is what makes me happy. By living, I mean experiencing new things, enjoying the things I like and not worrying about what in the end are trivial modern concerns. At fifty-one years old, I've had my share of heartbreaks (literally as well as figuratively) and disappointments, but I've also had amazing times and looking ahead, I don't want to get bogged down with normal life. I've only got a limited amount of time and spending it being happy seems to make perfect sense.

Later, after rereading those peculiar ramblings, I was in two minds whether to publish them. But having written the words it would have been churlish to leave them out. In the end this journal has been, is, and will continue to be an honest description of what I experience on the journey. The highs, the lows and the meditative in-between bits. I published it on my online blog once I got reconnected to the World Wide Web. How did we ever manage without it? Somehow we survived for millennia.

One footnote to add to this passage: after the racing, which saw a podium lockout by British riders, I visited the Ayrton Senna memorial, which is located at the spot where he died. While I am no big Formula One fan, it was a sombre moment, and the personal tributes placed there show how much impact that one person had on so many people. I don't think the visit to Imola would have been complete without visiting that spot.

Touring through Tuscany – Monday morning and I was up and packed at 7:30 and on the road by 8:30. After leaving Imola, I headed south-west towards Firenze. The English translation of the city's original name of Florentia is Florence. I don't know why we persist with that; it feels like something was lost in translation. I wanted to avoid using a motorway as usual and looking at a map I found a route that went over the hills towards the MotoGP circuit at Mugello, just north of Firenze. I found the cross-country road completely by accident once I set off. I turned out of the campsite away from the main road and immediately found a signpost with the correct road number on it... Destiny!

At the road's highest point, a cafe with a large parking area marks it out as a well-used motorcycle route and meeting place that is popular with local bikers. Linking the race circuits at Imola and Mugello like it does, I'm not surprised! Some fantastic hillside roads and stunning scenery provided an overload of riding entertainment for the day. Resting in the café car park, I chatted to a local guy riding a Triumph speed triple. It seems it is the place to go for the local bikers; no surprise there. The Triumph rider ran a safety school to educate bike riders on how to avoid becoming a statistic on the road's many tight curves. It seems local bikers throwing themselves at the scenery is a universal problem. Only five minutes later while looking at the said scenery I ran wide into a corner and gently brushed the roadside barrier. I had a bit of a word with myself after that and continued my journey with a little more care.

Dropping down out of the hills, the quiet roads are replaced by the bustling streets of Firenze. Scooters darting here and there, taking every opportunity to get to the front of queues, and every spare space on the street is taken up with gaggles of parked scooters of every description from the oldest 1960s Vespa to the latest twenty first century electric three-wheeled Yamaha. Ridden by businessmen, stylish girls and teenagers of every gender, it seems the way to get around the city is on a small powered two-wheeler. Taking a rest stop at a scenic viewpoint overlooking the Arno River and the Ponte Vecchio (lit: old bridge), famous for its jewellery shops, was a fantastic place to pause and take in the full sense of the historic city laid out below me. With the temperature gauge hitting 40°C it was time to shed a few layers and cool off as much as possible.

Heading out of Firenze, I followed signs towards Siena, along what promised to be a more interesting route than the autoroute, but it turned into a hot, dusty and rough road strewn with roadworks and infested with traffic. Keeping a look out for campsite signs proved to be a fruitless mission, and it was only when I got to the south of Siena that a peaceful countryside campsite provided a suitable antidote to my frazzled mind and body. Despite dropping the bike down a ditch while stationary before I set up the tent, it is a fabulous site with a vast array of stars on display in uninterrupted darkness. Standing naked in a deserted camping field in the middle of the night, staring at the stars, puts a human body into perspective. Time to recharge my own batteries and do some washing!

On Wednesday I retraced my steps through picture postcard Tuscany. Sun-blessed vineyards on the rolling hillsides, olive groves and medieval hilltop towns guided me to a day out in the glorious historic streets of Siena, which, legend has it, was founded by two sons of Remus, who was murdered by his brother Romulus, after whom Rome is named. Standing in the main Piazza del Campo, where the famous Palio horse race takes place each year, you get a real sense of the past that still lives in modern-day Italy, despite the hordes of tourists and associated businesses that feed off them. At €8 for a pistachio ice cream, they know how to make a living from it! It was, however, worth every cent!

I spent a little time on Thursday with a bit of motorcycle maintenance. The clutch had got a bit tight in the hot city traffic but was easily adjusted. The chain needs no adjustment at all so far, which bodes well. I am a little concerned at the wear rate of the tyres but will see how it goes. Not much I can do if they don't last to Istanbul as I originally planned, except buy some replacements if it comes to it. The first of my electrical failures occurred this week. My tablet stopped charging after the connection fell apart; one of my video cameras suffered the same fate. I set off with three video cameras. The first to fail was the most expensive. In fact, the cheapest Chinese eBay purchase went on to survive and record the whole journey!

A few blissful days basking in the peace and tranquillity of my Tuscan hillside campsite are perfect. Surrounded by nature, with the sounds of the woodland providing an incredibly restful setting, I made the mistake of leaving a half-eaten bowl of pasta outside my tent overnight and consequently found my collapsible camping bowl half-way down the hillside the next day with teeth puncture holes in it. Another piece of equipment I don't need any more. On Thursday the Dutch campsite owners provided a delicious evening meal of rolled tuna on lemon-dressed salad, followed by pasta with salmon, grated homegrown carrot and pine nuts.

After days of wonderful sunshine, it seems I have stayed too long in one place and the rain has found me again. Friday started with cloudy skies and light rain on the tent. 15°C feels a bit chilly now. I guess I'm getting acclimatised! A short journey brought me to the sulphurous hot springs of Saturnia, a regular tourist trap, it seems. Even for Italians it's a popular destination, but I can see why. The Romans, and before them the Etruscans, favoured the healing properties of the hot sulphurous spring waters. After 'taking the waters', I hope to report an improvement in my general health and well-being.

I spent the weekend doing a bit of shopping and browsing the stalls at the local town market in Arcidosso on Saturday. It felt cold today though, less than 10°C with a bit of rain. I needed extra layers on again. Sunday demands some pre-packing ahead of my next move. I'm heading for the west coast as I haven't seen the sea yet on this journey; time to rectify that. I'm aiming for somewhere near Grosseto for a few days before moving a little further north, but staying near the coast over next weekend, then somewhere near Firenze until Friday, when I have a hotel booked for the Mugello MotoGP weekend. Nothing is eternal on the road. It is always time to move on.

Apart from that preparation, I'm not planning on doing very much; the sun is shining and time to relax a little ahead of my next travelling adventure. I'm not sure I have ever had this much contemplation time, or just time full stop. A holiday is a break from work. This journey is a break from life! I have lots of time to think about what's important, what's not and what makes me happy. Right now, I really think I need to change a few things when I get back, perhaps move house, be different. It's an amazing feeling to have space in my thoughts to think clearly. No confusion, no one to influence those thoughts. Not that I am overly influenced, but it feels clear. Riding my bike as I travel, moving from place to place. Homeless in a way, but not, always moving but still me, a purity and distillation of who I am. I am missing a little human contact, easy communication and pointless chat in my own language. However well someone speaks English, the subtleties of native speakers are lost in the same way that my own pathetic attempts at language will never be even close to fluent.

'RESTLESS' – **Blackberry Smoke**

Not that I'm searching for something out here, but I like the song and it fits the mood. Keep on rolling baby.

Coastal camping – An easy day, riding about 50km brought me to the west coast, just south of a few of the less-than pleasing seaside towns in the Grossetto region. A few dead-end roads to one-horse towns led me astray for a while, but after miles of endless caravan estates I stumbled across the picturesque little seaside village of Porto Ercole. After a fruitless trip along a hillside road that degenerated to a gravel track, I backtracked and discovered the local campsite, which had its share of permanently moored touring vans, but a shady spot under tall pine trees at the back of the site for tents. Va bene, grazie, even if I can't connect to your free Wi-Fi. After pasta with tuna, tomatoes and olives plus half a bottle of Chianti in the company of a small herd of inquisitive deer, the night passed by without disturbance.

On Tuesday morning I took a wander along the expansive length of beach. Getting away from the bars and managed area, the natural beach with large amounts of driftwood stacked up to the dunes by wave action was more than a match for the raked and tidied areas of the umbrella-populated entrance.

Taking a siesta out of the midday sun under the tall pines, I have decided to move on tomorrow and head somewhere a little north to stay over the weekend. While seeing the sea is a pleasant change of scenery, the thought of lots of Italians descending on the current oasis of peace isn't one I cherish. The coast just south of Livorno might prove interesting, or not. Change isn't always better, but it is always different. If an endless stream of static touring caravans is the flavour of the day, I might head inland a little. At least that area does put me back in easy reach of Pisa, for that gratuitous tower shot that I missed a couple of weeks ago. In the afternoon I took the short trip to Orbetello, a small island town in the middle of a lake established in 280BC that provided a base for a German float plane squadron during World War Two. While contemplating the cool waters surrounding the town, I met Marco, an Italian guy travelling around the coastline of Italy by bike over the next few months. Back at the campsite, an evening's discussion about the Italian MotoGP stars brought the day to an end.

Wednesday saw me get as far as Marina Di Castagneto, a small village right on the coast. A large family campsite that is mostly unpopulated at this time of year provides a decent resting place for a while, the sound of the sea easing me to sleep. Piombino didn't hold much interest other than being a port town for the short trip to Elba. A brief stop at the ancient Etruscan town of Populonia looked interesting, but local camping was a bit thin on the ground. I'm planning on stopping by while I'm in the area. There is also (on Marco's recommendation) a castle at Bolgheri which was worth a visit as well.

Thursday is a day for catching up with some housekeeping, washing, shopping, all the day-to-day stuff that still has to happen even in the completely non-normal way of life that I have now. But the sun is shining, the sound and scent of the ocean fills the air while I wash the breakfast pots and plan the rest of the day without even knowing what time it is. I don't wear a watch because to me it lets the wearer see every second of life ticking away. Sunshine, daylight and my internal clock telling me it's time to eat is enough of a time check. There is no timetable to keep to or schedules to be met. Life is simple and that's fine, thanks. Strange dreams filled the night and life seemed a little unreal first thing in the morning. Manoeuvring the bike, I managed to overbalance and tip it over onto its side next to the tent, which brought me back to reality with a crash. The day also started with the failure of my iPod, which meant I was music-less. It was working fine the night before, just another electrical casualty. Luckily, I managed to save the music to my computer despite Apple's best efforts to make it as difficult as possible to sync up one of their devices with a Microsoft Windows machine.

My Azerbaijani visa arrived by email as well. I just have to find a way of printing it out. It is just as well that I'm relaxed about my timetable as a rainy day meant I could take the day off. There's not much point going out and getting wet. One disadvantage of a bike and tent combination, I guess. However, the day was not lost as I spent it reading my latest book, raiding my food stores and enjoying the sound of rain on the tent.

I realised today is one month to the day since I left Britain's grey shores for, at the time, even darker lands. But, since those initial three difficult days, life has been good, living in the warmth of Italy. Good food, good wine and relaxed times, moving when I want to, travelling when I feel the need and staying still because I can. Next weekend I travel to Mugello to fulfil the long-held ambition to see the Italian MotoGP round. I hope it lives up to expectations! After that, I head south to tackle more of this adventure. Another holiday destination perhaps, but one I have never sampled so I have no preconceptions. Do I take in the popular tourist destinations? Probably not; I never really have, so there's no point starting now.

After six days by the sea I feel a need to move, and tomorrow I will travel inland a little way. I guess I'm more of a country boy than a seafarer at heart. After two hours packing up the tent I set off inland towards Cecina and Volterra, which provided an entertaining ride along wonderfully scenic roads, arriving at the walled medieval hill town of San Gimignano, known for its well-preserved towers built during two centuries of local family rivalries.

A campsite just outside town provides all the accommodation I need. There's a few more issues with my kit and bike that I need to address. It's becoming a bit of a maintenance overhead, but if I want the bike to make it all the way I guess I need to stay on top of the little things to avoid those becoming big issues. My sleeping bag has ripped, so a needle and cotton was brought into play. The headlight bulb on the bike has blown. That's nothing unusual, so a replacement from a garage sorted it out. An irritating vibration from the fairing panel got annoying enough for me to fix it. It was probably a consequence of an earlier inept maintenance job by me that left it not properly secured anyway.

A twenty-minute walk into town earned me a treat

of beer and a pizza in the main square, although I forgot that pepperoni in Italy is a pepper or capsicum and not the spicy meat sausage I was expecting. It's continuously amusing how there's no apparent rush to life in Italy. The waitress took her time delivering my order to the table. An Italian couple sat at the table next to me took almost as long over a coffee as I did eating a pizza. The British sense of personal space getting squished, a bit of a shower of rain while I eat and an old Italian woman shelters under my table's umbrella. A spot of tourist-watching is an amusing pastime. Americans in a group with a tour guide: "Oh my god; it's SO amazing!" and Germans by the hoard laying claim to tables and confiscating chairs. A retirement-aged British couple at the street cafe ordered food after which she went to the ladies'. In the meantime the waitress delivered a ham sandwich and two coffees. The guy was eating when she returned and she asked where her food was. He replied it was very nice anyway and scoffed the lot, while she complained at him but didn't call the waitress back to tell her there was something missing. Britons don't do complaining very well. San Gimignano is a wonderful place. All it takes is a little exploration and it's easy to get away from the crowds of tourists. Find a little secluded space on the ancient walls and just immerse myself in the wonderful views and fabulous Italian atmosphere.

After a few wonderful days soaking up the perfect Tuscan scenery it's time to move on. My destination is a little hotel on the outskirts of Firenze and I collected the 2015 Mugello MotoGP tickets on the way. Come on England! Can British riders Cal Crutchlow, Brad Smith, and Scott

Redding and Irishman Eugene Laverty do us proud? I hope so!

Madness, mayhem and motorbikes, Mugello – Well, to start at the end, I've given up getting out of circuit after the race for a while, so found a shady spot to let the departing hoards pass me by while I reflect on the whole event. Where to start describing this experience in words is beyond my vocabulary. Take a rock concert, throw in lots of very loud motorbikes both on and off track. Chuck in a whole population of crazy Italians. Braze gently under a hot sun and add large amounts of alcohol. Mix together with smoked barbecued food, add smoke bombs and burnt out tyres then stir loudly with a manic chainsaw, scooters with no exhausts and booming Ducati motorcycles revved to the limiter. Maybe I'm almost getting the image across. Everything that the Imola World superbike meeting wasn't, this is and much, much more.

Every day is a race on Italy's public roads, but this morning was the world championship event, with everything from sports bikes to tourers, scooters to adventure bikes out to overtake everyone else on the way to the race. I arrived on race day by 8.30am but the party had already started. I guess it never actually stopped from Saturday night! Camping is a free-for-all once you're in and everything from expensive campers to throwaway tents compete for every spare space, making use of even the most unlikely camping spots.

After the race I joined the melee on the track under the grandstand to see the podium and an unpopular Spanish winner in Jorge Lorenzo. A great race and the British riders did well despite a late crash for Cal Crutchlow.

An update on the Mugello exit strategy while I write this all down. There isn't one! I expected chaos and I wasn't disappointed. An hour and a half after making my way towards the exit I eventually got there only to find the road utterly gridlocked for over an hour. So another sit in the shade until some traffic movement occurs. To be followed by the polizia closing the road I needed to get back to the hotel. A very helpful policeman suggested an alternative route that took me an hour to get to a point ten minutes down the road from where I left the circuit. Italian organisation at its best! The journey back into Firenze was a fun ride surrounded by a mass convoy of bikes of all denominations.

Back in the city, I took a leisurely stroll into the central Piazza della Signoria in search of a little culture and entertainment. With copies of Michelangelo's David and other work on display by classical Italian artists mostly recognised as mutant turtles by the younger generation, the hustle and bustle of a modern tourist hotspot was a great place to savour the atmosphere and enjoy a pistachio ice cream before getting lost among the narrow streets on my way back to my little hotel.

So after the madness of Mugello it is time to head further south and explore the heel of Italy as I head south to catch a boat across the Ionian Sea. I'm currently in no mind to rush and don't intend to push for a lot of miles each day. So I'll see what I find and where I end up along the way.

Southern sunsets – Winding my way through the narrow historic streets of Firenze with the thermometer on my bike showing more than 30°C, I happened across a couple two up on a 1989 G-registered air cooled BMW R80GS. As they pulled up at the next set of red traffic lights, I pulled up alongside and with easy communication, aided by my flip-up crash helmet, said, "Hello." The pillion asked where I was headed. I had time to shout I was heading for Arezzo before the lights changed to green. As I got to the next lights first, the rider stayed behind me, obviously nothing more to say. At the next junction they passed me without a wave and went straight on when I turned off. I guess some people just don't like to talk.

The Umbrian regional capital of Perugia came and went and wasn't missed in its passing as I headed for the hills in search of scenic routes. While looking for an exit from the city, a chap on a Yamaha T-Max 500cc scooter waved me to a stop as I turned off the motorway. Without any common language between us we had a chat about my route and where I should go next in the area. I guess some people do like to talk after all.

Picking up a road into the Apennines, the scenery got decidedly mountainous as it twisted and turned towards the sky. Late in the day I had nearly given up on finding a campsite when, as I turned around to go back to the last little hilltop town of Cascia where I had seen hotels, a sign for camping caught my eye. Something has a habit of turning up when you need it most. Maybe that's just me? A lovely, peaceful campsite in the cool evening air was just the tonic I needed after a hot day. Sitting on the pool terrace, sipping a cold glass of beer with a bowl of pasta. The warm glow of an impressive sunset easing me into the evening.

Heading further south the next day, I missed what

appeared to be some popular biking routes as scores of sports bikes passed me in both directions en route to more interesting curves than the road I travelled along. The coastal route looked promising on a map but proved less interesting as fresh mountain air gave way to overpopulated, uninspiring coastal towns. Further south still, the land is significantly different to the Italy I have loved so far. Drier, less green, with cacti and faded signs pointing the route along crumbling roads lined with rubbish at every pull-in area. In search of more salubrious surroundings, I headed into the Gargano National Park.

Getting away from the coast, a hillside campsite under the shade of some huge conifers was a nice place to spend a couple of nights as I caught up with some housekeeping. At €33 a night, it was the most expensive site I stayed at in Italy; it wasn't worth that much. At least my washing dried quickly in the heat of the day. An evening meal in the campsite bar was finished off with my first very pleasant experience of mulberries. I also adjusted the chain on the bike for the first time since I departed England. Quite amazing given the distances I've travelled so far. Not for the first time, though, I had to adjust the clutch again as it started dragging in the heat. I had replaced the clutch plates before I left, but it seems to struggle with hot temperatures, which doesn't bode well for what's to come. My last night in Italy was spent pre-packing the panniers to allow me to get a relatively early start as I head for the port to take the trip to my next chapter.

The last day in Italy saw me on a road out of the Parco Nazionale del Gargano that proved to be a tight, twisty affair as I navigated around a coach that had got beached on one particularly sharp curve, with the front up against the roadside barrier and the back end grounded on the road. That was at least an interesting route, whereas the road through what is laughingly called the Rivera, which included a lot of run-down and dilapidated campsites and industrial townships, was straight, uninteresting and badly surfaced. In an effort to 'just get there' I hit the autostrada towards Bari, where a boat bound for Greece was waiting patiently.

In a final flourish of Italian organisation, the official managing the boarding of vehicles blew his whistle and pointed at me to board, before almost losing the pea out of said whistle as he got me to stop before I reached the ramp onto the boat. Thereafter, he made me wait under the baking sun until almost everyone else was on board. I'm sure there was a joke there somewhere, but I missed it.

The Italian job is done. Arrivederci, Italia. Ciao.

5 GREECE – KALIMÉRA

The overnight ferry bound for Patras meant getting what sleep I could on a bench seat in the cabin before the scheduled 4.30am arrival; it might be a long night and day. Sadly, sleep was off the menu for a troupe of Hell's Angels from all points of the compass drinking the ship's bar dry and singing their way through the night, still with pints of lager in hand early in the morning. "Brother!" with a thumb handshake and a slap on the back, it seems, is the greeting between clans. Chill out, guys; life isn't that much of a competition.

Arrival was a simple affair with no passport checks. Still in Europe, after all. At least they are still in the euro, which given that I have a reserve of euros with me is a good thing! Wasn't sure they would be by the time I got here. Arriving in the early hours meant waiting for the world to wake up. A pre-dawn ride to the beach was peaceful, and sitting on a sea wall contemplating the clear, calm waters was a wonderfully relaxing introduction to the Greek way of life. Turning away from the sea, I rode up the nearest hill to get the lay of the land. At the highest point, the view over the bay at sunrise was stunning. A derelict holiday home provided a place to sit back and watch the day dawn and allowed me an hour's snooze until it got hot.

An olive tree-shaded campsite at €10 a night is my introduction to Greece. The cheapest night so far and I swiftly fell asleep at 3pm! In the cooler evening I strolled down to the beach to replace my old faithful sunglasses that disappeared somewhere on the last part of the journey. I don't pay a lot for sunglasses because I invariably lose them or break them, but the last pair I had grown rather fond of as I had owned them since the last time I attended a superbike race in Italy in 2002.

The next day was spent with a bit more bike maintenance. The drive chain seemed a bit noisy, but adjusted okay, and with some additional lubrication it appears to be all right. I found a replacement MP3 player for my dead iPod and went for a swim to cool off in the heat of the afternoon: a pastime that would become a daily ritual in the area. Later I decided to sort out my riding gear a bit. The textile jacket and trousers are too much in 30°C heat, even with the air vents fully open, and it's going to get hotter than this. There is a balance between safety and comfort. Safety is important, but so is being able to concentrate without being boiled alive. Riding in shorts and flip-flops might be acceptable to holidaying tourists on rented scooters, but the consequences of an 'off' are over the threshold for me. For years I rode a bike with just a leather jacket and denim jeans and that is the minimum for me. I managed to survive teenage years without too many scrapes when that was the extent of my riding equipment. That's what is going to work for me now. With my flip-front helmet open it is a very satisfying way to ride my bike around beach front areas.

I need to press on a bit as my Kazakhstani visa starts on the 13th of July and I need to be at the Russian border for the start of that visa at the beginning of August to have enough time to get to Vladivostok before it expires. So I have a limited amount of time to get through Greece, Turkey, Georgia and Azerbaijan. One thing I was trying to avoid was to be tied to deadlines on this journey, but the need for visas has made that a necessity. That's the way of it, so I just have to suck it up and go with the flow. Just need to cover some miles.

Sadly, my Turkish tyre supplier has informed me via email that he can't get the tyres I wanted to cross Kazakhstan now, and seeing as I sold the pair I had before I left, rather than carry them across Europe, it leaves me with a bit of a dilemma. The tyres I've got, I am now confident will last until Istanbul. Quite a recommendation for a 'rain tyre' given the heat they've been subjected to. Their finishing mileage will be interesting once I know it. For now, a bottle of cheap red, some strange spicy olive paste and crusty bread make life sweet. It's gonna get hotta!

Greece seems easier than Italy so far. The drivers aren't quite as mad, the food and wine are fascinating, the sea is clear although the sun is fierce at midday and I need to find some shade. I think I will need to travel earlier in the day and later in the afternoon. I could do with a couple of nights in one spot to find my feet a bit. 'It's all Greek' now has a whole new meaning. Luckily, English is spoken almost everywhere so far. Efharisto!

Olympic origins – As the seat of the Greek gods and the birthplace of civilisation, the land of package holiday dreams, endless sunshine, big skies and huge scenery, I can understand why so many fall in love with this country.

Like anywhere, there are good and bad bits, but the good are amazing! Crystal clear sea lapping against hot sandy shorelines is a difficult combination to beat.

Not much sign to this passing traveller of the financial woes this country is suffering, but I haven't got access to twenty-four hour news channels that need to fill empty airtime, not that I want it! Taking the main route across country meant using a toll road, but just over €5 to cross from the west coast to the east is acceptable for me.

With the Aegean gently rolling against the land, I have found a place to kick back for a while. Getting across Greece is not the big distances I had thought, and I'm taking a little time out. I could be in Turkey by the weekend, but I'm of a mind to explore a bit more of this coast. I'm not far from the three-pronged Chalkidiki peninsular, and I'm loving swimming in wonderful, clear seawater. With plenty of desert ahead I'm making the most of it.

I don't yet know what Turkey has in store but as a holiday destination Greece is idyllic. I know some will see this whole trip as one long holiday and in some respects it is, but the endless moving on demands a bit of downtime for me; that way it works. I can find a spot and get to know it a little and feel almost at home. It positively charges me for the next challenge. Failing to find a fast enough internet connection to upload some video to YouTube, it is time for a swim. It's tough but someone's gotta do it. Might as well be me!

Crystal Aegean contemplation – I found a campsite and just stopped, not going any further today. Nice temperatures at 28°C; cool, clear sea; and a bar stocked with cold beer. Not moving! On the second day, I've gone to the beach! I'm going to hang around here till after the weekend. Although the road back from this beachfront is fairly small, I think covering the miles will be fine once I get back to the main road and head into Turkey. I've still got time and I'm enjoying the peaceful relaxation of Greece; it feels laid-back and easy-going. Everyone speaks English and maybe I'm just avoiding moving on for a while, but it's a great place to be. I've got the tarpaulin that I've used to create extra space on the front of my tent, but it works very well as a beach sunshade.

Hot again today, over 30°C and I can't quite raise the enthusiasm for pulling on hot textile trousers and jacket, taking another day. Looking at the map, I can get to the Turkish border in about a day's ride if I push on, but for now I'm going to move around the coast here a bit. Travelling in jeans and denim jacket, not the most protective of travel clothing, but then I am very much overdressed compared to the locals in flip-flops and shorts. There is a balance, and staying cooler helps with concentration, that is for sure. There will be times when I will have to grin and bear it. Travelling across barren rock-strewn landscapes will demand that level of protection, but cruising around the coast I've taken a leaf out of the locals' book: travel cool, just don't fall off!

I didn't get very far the next day either, only round the coast to Kalamisti. White sand and a campsite that almost touches the beach, more crystal blue sea and the usual flotilla of pleasure boats that all conspired to pull me off the hot tarmac and refused to let me go. I'm not trying very hard to resist. Another day and I travelled as far as the beach, sat under the shade of my tarp, swam in the clear sea, soaked up the sun and wandered back to the tent. That's far enough, thanks. A bar has Wi-Fi and I can at least update my online blog. All internet connection in Greece seems to be via satellite, which can be a bit on the slow side.

I'm not sure if I'm being reluctant to leave Greece or not. I think I am a bit. It's comfortable. It's warm and sunny. It is one big holiday and I know that things will get tougher as I go further east. So I think I'm making the most of it while I can. Plus I think I had a bit too much sun yesterday; I feel a bit lightheaded today. Not travelling far.

I have decided that I will get to the Turkish border by next weekend and push on from there. I think that the north coast of Turkey will be a bit cooler to travel and put some miles in once I've sorted out replacing the tyres at the shop near Istanbul that I have been in touch with before I departed England. It is actually quite a bit south of Istanbul, so I hope I will be able to bypass the major centre of traffic chaos.

With all this relaxed contemplation, I thought it worth updating my state of mind. I know that after the Imola weekend I seemed a bit melancholy about missing things about my normal life. A lot of those feelings were brought about, I think, by the slight disappointment I felt by the world superbike event and the lack of atmosphere not matching my expectations. Mugello made up for that and lots of experiences since have made me realise what it is I'm doing here. Yes, some of it isn't easy, some of it is tough. Some of it challenges what I think I am capable of and who I am. But some of it, like this place, makes me realise how amazing the whole experience is as it stretches out in front of me with so much more to come. Moving on… soon.

My final night in Greece was spent at a quiet campsite near Alexandroupoli, which has a mixed history being so close to Turkey and Bulgaria. I shared the spacious site with a lone Dutch cyclist. We were the only occupants, the site owner at pains to point out the government's inability to fund development of a potentially lucrative tourist area with ancient Greek sites and artefacts all nearby, the usual tourist hotspots further west taking the lion's share of the tourist euro.

> I know not how I seem to others,
> but to myself I am but a small child
> wandering upon the vast shores of knowledge,
> every now and then finding a small bright pebble
> to content myself with while the vast
> ocean of undiscovered truth lies before me.
>
> **– Plato**

6 TURKEY – HOŞ BULDUK

Arriving at the Turkish border by 9.30am gave me time to prepare for what would be my first proper border crossing: one that required passport and document checks. An amazing situation to think about really, having travelled all the way from home without actually needing a passport through four different countries. Crossing into country number five, I think I've found a rhythm to travelling. The border crossing itself was relatively easy, about an hour of document checks and double checks and triple checks, but at least they didn't want to unpack all my bags, which they did with a few cars. The border guard took a look at the mass of disorganised baggage strapped to my bike and baulked at the idea, I think.

Covering the miles is no problem; it gives me time to watch the scenery change from rolling hills and mountainous regions to flat farmland or urban areas. It gives me time to think clearly, or time to just relax and enjoy the feel of riding my bike. The rhythmic beat of its two-cylinder engine providing a baseline to the feel of the wind and the sun. Open to the elements and at one with the world. Camping is a ritual of unpacking and repacking. My daily list of 'needs' consists of three things: fuel in the tank, somewhere to sleep and something to eat. Life doesn't get much less complicated than that. It's become my eternal triangle.

Greece was a fabulous place to be. From what I have seen of Turkey so far, it is very different. As with Greece, away from the tourist areas life is not one long holiday town and near the nether regions of country borders it's downright ugly. I suffered culture shock on arrival, but I think that's true whenever you enter a new country and I expect it will be bigger the further east I go. But get away from the dirt and grime that seems to stick like shit to lines on a map, or the shiny tourist hotpots, and you find the real country. The real people and a true sense of what a country is.

With my large scale paper map lacking any useful details, satellite navigation on my smartphone came into play as I headed towards Gallipoli to take a boat across the Dardanelles. I expected an historic wartime Ottoman Empire remembrance, where thousands of ANZAC soldiers died without a military victory. I got messy modern chaos. After crossing the river to Lapseki with the bike wedged between trucks and cars on a chugging tub of a river ferry, I followed the coast to reach Bandirma by mid-afternoon, where my tyre replacements were waiting. My initial thoughts of where the bike shop was when I made contact with the owner were a little off. I had imagined it was close to Istanbul, when in fact it is 250km away in Bandirma, which sits on the south coast of the Sea of Marmara, while Istanbul sits on the north coast of the same inland sea.

A little later in the day than anticipated, I got new tyres fitted. Actually, only one new tyre fitted, a more off-road-orientated Continental TKC80 on the rear. The front is still hardly worn after 7000km; the rear was actually still serviceable. A real tribute to supposedly soft compound Heidenau rain tyres and at £130 for the pair I can highly recommend them. I'm now equipped and have a little more off-road capability. It feels like I will be able to deal with what comes next. The guys in the bike shop were amusingly familiar. Despite the lack of English they were not much different from a UK backstreet bike shop, oblivious to the low-level Turkish Air Force manoeuvres overhead and chain-smoking their way through fitting my tyre.

Sat in a hotel room with a loudspeaker calling the devoted to prayer, competing with Arabian rhythms from a particularly loud stereo system, cars and bikes hooting at each other, the sound of ships in the harbour and fragrant smells of kebab and spices wafting in on the hot night air feels much more like a foreign country than any European travel has so far. A seventh-floor room with an open patio door that steps straight into thin air without a barrier provided a sense of vertigo to add to the sense of displacement. A streetside café's meat kebab dish with yoghurt and chilli eased me into the evening. The culture shock has relaxed a little and I'm ready to take the next step on my journey around our little blue planet.

I haven't been able to upload any video to my YouTube channel. I'm getting so far behind that although I want to publish them in chronological order so they make sense, it's become something of a task. Now if I had a film crew with me… hmm. Maybe that would lose the effect of my out-of-focus or out-of-shot film production. Being the director, cameraman and subject means I get it wrong more often than I get it right, but that's part of the charm. I hope!

So while the Turkish nightlife kicks off, this particular weary traveller is kicking back for tonight. A hot day's riding, from watching a glorious sunrise in Greece this morning to an equally impressive sunset over the harbour in western Turkey, is enough sensory input for one day in a journey that is a constant stream of experience.

Turkish delight – Thursday saw my biggest day riding so far, to get from Bandirma, where I replaced the tyre, to the Black Sea coast at Amasra. I spent most of the day with one or two of my triangle pieces complete, fuel and food on board. Heading towards the coast, I wasn't concerned about finding accommodation and I was right. 525km in one day saw me across the hills that separate the north and the middle of Turkey. The roads varied from new motorways, to worn-out dual carriageways, broken down tarmac roads and plain rutted gravel. Some were half built and some were half ruined. The motorways had automatic toll booths where I triggered alarms as I passed, my bike registration not registered!

Likewise, the countryside was dramatic. In places hot and dry, arid land littered with human detritus which gave way to softer, greener landscapes as I climbed into the hills, followed by views of the brooding Black Sea. The traffic went from modern cars, coaches and trucks in the more affluent areas to older flagging Fiats, FSOs and wrecked Renaults. The temperatures varied from a fearsome 38°C over the flatlands to a chilly 15°C in the mountain rain and a comfortable 20°C on the coast. Ying and yang.

Most Turks don't seem to feel the need to clear up

their rubbish, it seems. The countryside appears to offer a multitude of opportunities to dispose of everything from building rubble to household waste. In contrast, it also seems to offer a million opportunities to plant a huge Turkish flag, lest you forget where you are. It's a shame such national pride isn't reflected in their respect for the natural world.

After a pleasant overnight in a little backstreet hotel at the picturesque seaside town of Amasra, the day started with a breakfast of smoked luncheon meat, hard-boiled eggs and black olives, accompanied by the loud shudders of a thunderstorm. But by mid-morning I was travelling the Black Sea coastal road under a wonderful clear blue sky. A lot of the scenery felt like being in North Wales, with wooded hillsides soaring above a blue-green sea and stony beaches, the road twisting and turning through valleys and over hills. It needs care, though, because the tarmac surface was once again a long way on its journey back to nature. Rutted and rippled on the way into a corner, littered with gravel on the apex and slick, smooth, worn tarmac on the exit. Most bike riders' worst nightmare, my new off-road rear tyre offering less confidence than the tyre it replaced. The fun level is still set to maximum, though!

While taking a brief rest stop, contemplating the meaning of life and admiring the view over the calm Black Sea, while ignoring yet more household waste, a BMW rider whizzed around the corner and drew to a stop in a cloud of dust and a flurry of excitement. The German rider who didn't share his name with me was overflowing with positivity. Asking where I was going. Telling me he was on his way home from Mongolia. With broken spokes on his wheel that he hoped would not collapse before he got back to Germany. Still on the tyres with which he had set off on his journey. A flash of expensive camera from the tank bag of his bike to record the moment and he was gone with a wave and a grin. That brief encounter made me smile for the rest of the day as his positive excitement cast a sharp spotlight on one of my quieter moments.

By late afternoon I had reached the historic port of Sinop, a town with a certain craggy charm and the remains of ancient fortifications. It is a place full of ancient history and folklore. Alleged to have been founded by a companion of Hercules, it has been an important fishing port for centuries. While modern shops huddle together on the busy main street, the seafront is packed with fishing boats crowded together on the docksides and rows of ships propped up for repairs on dry dock blocks. A campsite by the sea on the leeward side of Sinop's isthmus provided the night's accommodation for the equivalent of about £7.

A confluence of journeys – Travelling east along the coast, I had set Trabzon as an achievable destination for the day. While looking at the map I had for Turkey, it looked a short distance, but the scale of the map flattered to deceive. The road was good and smooth-going; however, my more off-road-orientated new rear tyre was less happy and the increase in vibration and noise was becoming a less pleasing aspect of the chunky tread pattern. I covered the considerable distance easily on the good road; however, Trabzon was not worth stopping at and I moved on towards Rize.

One connection I had made while planning my trip was with Stuart, a retired fireman who was travelling with a companion to Mongolia. It seemed they would be taking a similar route to mine along the north coast of Turkey, heading for Baku in Azerbaijan. I had heard from Stuart on my arrival in Turkey as their route brought them overland through Eastern Europe. Riding the road towards Rize, I spotted two Yamaha Xt660s parked up in a side road. Stuart and Olly were chatting to a local biker. We rode into the town together, and after a few enquiries with a group of old gents playing dominoes on a streetside café we headed to the recommended 'grin' hotel, which actually turned out to be the Green Hotel. Quite a posh place in this little town and the price of the rooms dictated a shared accommodation. An evening's wander among the quiet streets provided an evening meal of kebab and meat stew with no alcohol on the menu anywhere, including the hotel bar area, locals sipping strong tea while they chatted loudly over cards or tiles on tables outside cafes. My first experience of eastern cultural influences on this trip.

Turkey is a land of big contrasts. Some amazing, some less so! The people I've met seem genuinely friendly. While I'm sure there's lots to see if you were to take the time, I am just pushing on for now. My Azerbaijani visa starts in six days and my Kazakhstani visa twelve days after that, so it's time to travel through this land and see its virtues as I pass by, which actually is probably for the best, because if you look too closely it is less appealing. A bit like the famous sweet: initially sweet and sugar-coated, but strangely sickly and less cohesive underneath.

7 GEORGIA – K'ETILI IQ'OS TKVEN

I'm not so much a Georgia satellite, more a surface rover as I landed in Georgia via a simple border crossing. First impressions of Georgia are good as it seems like a nice place to be, with beautiful countryside. The small towns and villages that the wide road passes through have an air of a country doing well. Modern shops and plenty of expensive-looking cars parked in the streets around Batumi. There are lots of Judge Dredd-style Ford police special patrol cars with blue and red lights lit at all times patrolling every stretch of road and several cars being pulled over for checks or minor traffic infringements.

Having hooked up with Stuart and Olly, who are heading to Mongolia, we are travelling in the same direction for a while. We camped on the first night on a grassy dune next to the beach just south of the port town of Poti, which is home to what passes as the Georgian navy. A thunderstorm overnight didn't disturb me, despite my gentle teasing of Stuart setting up his tent thoroughly while my lackadaisical preparations proved a little lacking later in the night. A local police officer decided we were worth investigating but after a little chat, where I learnt a few Georgian words, he just parked overnight nearby until we left the next morning. I'm not sure if he was providing security or taking the opportunity to avoid other more taxing duties. It was a little strange but hey, we left the area tidier than when we arrived!

Tbilisi beckons on day two. Stuart and Olly wanted to press on across the whole country to Tbilisi, the destination seeming more important than the journey. I tagged along, which was okay, but meant that I relinquished my pleasurable pace and ease of stopping anywhere that caught my interest. The journey, though, was interesting, as we passed through mountains and valleys. Quiet villages that appeared to remain mostly oblivious to the twenty-first century, with old fellas watching the world as it passed by their front door. Out in the countryside there seem to be lots of people stood by the roadside. I don't know how long they've been waiting for that bus, but some of them have grown old during the wait. Arriving in Tbilisi, it was being baked on the grass steppe under a cloudless sky, hotter than a hot thing on a hot day. Even the air is turned up to eleven. 40°C feels like a furnace blast in my open-face helmet with the visor lifted even if I thought I had acclimatised to warmer temperatures a bit.

Checking my Azerbaijani visa shows me I got things a bit wrong with the dates. I will now stay in Tbilisi until Monday, when my visa starts, which gives a few days to explore this city a bit. While the modern bits are not the prettiest city in the world, it must have some olde worlde charm away from the madness of the road system and battling traffic. I just need to uncover it somehow. At least it's a very cheap place to live. The hotel is £8 a night, petrol at about 60p a litre and beer at not much more. There is some affluence in this city, though, new BMWs and Mercedes rubbing shoulders (quite literally in most cases) with old battered cars missing body parts, but still labouring on beyond reasonable use.

Walking during the hottest part of the day like typically English madmen, in a fruitless search of the old town alongside the Kura River, Stuart, Olly and I spent a sweaty couple of hours in search of the elusive prettier parts of the town until we found a green square with a bar and sat for a while watching the world go by. A taxi ride back to the hotel showed up the local driving habits first-hand. No mercy asked or given! But I've got used to what initially felt like suicidal overtakes, undertakes, queue-jumping and impatience because the driver at the front of the queue actually waited for the lights to turn green! It's all good, it all works somehow. Just like the ramshackle buildings that somehow remain standing despite huge cracks in the brickwork.

A recent flood is the news headline banner as a clean-up operation is underway. Dozens of workers pulling debris from the river, which I have read has been deliberately lowered to enable the search for any victims. A grim task! The other signs of the flood are large deposits of dried mud encasing whole cars and the ruins of the zoo on the banks of a stream that obviously provided the conduit for flood waters rushing down to the river. No sign of any escaped tigers, though!

I will also take the opportunity to change some money to universally accepted US dollars before I move on. From Wednesday I'm back to being on my own, which is not so bad. I like making my own decisions and taking my own direction, stopping when I want and moving when I choose.

Stationary in Tbilisi – After realising my Azerbaijani visa is not valid until Monday the 6th — I have a chance to explore Tbilisi a bit more. I have been glad for the opportunity because I'm sure I would have left here thinking there was nothing to see. While large parts of this city are made up of wide, fast-flowing chaotic roads populated by everything from new Mercedes to lowered and loud Japanese racers, to clapped-out Russian jalopies all in a daily wacky race, there is much more. Freedom Square has a golden statue of St George that replaced an earlier carving of Lenin's head. It celebrates Georgian independence atop a column that would have made Nelson jealous. Nearby, the older part of town has tree-lined and cobbled shady streets, occupied by a plethora of small shops selling everything from wines and silver to local food products and tourist souvenirs. Cafes provide local food and a place to sit away from the day's heat. There is also a very modern out-of-town shopping centre that would not look out of place anywhere in affluent Europe, with cars on display in the main foyer. The flood appears to have closed a few roads, which may to some extent explain my experience of the busy roads, but a lot of clean-up work is in progress.

Georgia has had a troubled past and only a few years ago Russia threatened invasion again. But modern Georgian people seem incredibly friendly and there is a sense of good times despite the UK government's travel advice. My next destination may provide more in the way of a culture shock as I move from Georgia's mostly European feel to a country with a well-publicised corruption problem. But I hope, like most places I have passed through, that the fear of getting there is worse than the actual experience of being there. We shall see.

In the meantime I'm going to indulge my curiosity and spend the weekend enjoying Tbilisi Old Town, still trying to not giggle when I say thank you in Georgian which is pronounced 'mad lover'... little things!

Decisions made – I'm staying in Georgia for a while. No point crossing the border into Azerbaijan at the moment. I've read and been told of numerous issues in Azerbaijan. While I'm not one to worry too much about other people's experiences, recent reports have suggested it's not an easy place to be. With my Kazakhstani visa not valid until the 13th of July I would effectively be stuck in Baku for a week. My mistake while applying for the visa dates, but hey, I didn't know better at the time. Travel is an education amongst other things. I have also been advised that the authorities only give seventy-two hour vehicle permits on entry whatever the entry visa says, so it all makes sense to sit tight for a while and travel to Azerbaijan once I have an exit strategy.

In the meantime, living is cheap in Tbilisi. It's a bit of a pain living in a city as, a country boy at heart, I miss the open space, but it is what it is and I'll move on Monday to a place close to the Old Town where I can relax and set myself up for the next stage. Walking around the city, I have found lots of interesting places and investigated a bit of the heritage of the place. There are sharp contrasts between rich and poor, from new Mercedes to beggars on the street. Crossing the road is like playing a real-life version of the classic 1980s Frogger arcade game, but waiting for the traffic to stop even with a green crossing light isn't going to happen. Just go for it and dodge the cars/vans/buses/trucks across a six-lane road... easy!

If I was sat in a campsite in the country I would be happy to stay put for as long as it takes, but a hotel room in the city isn't my idea of fun. I've looked around and seen the sights. It's a case of sitting it out, checking out the local cafes and browsing the shops. I've hardly spent any money in the last week and I don't see that changing much. I need to do a little bit of maintenance on the bike, but will sort that out next week. One other decision I have made is that I will take the more northern border crossing. It sounds far more interesting than the motorway/main road option further south. I've pre-booked a small hotel in Baku for next weekend until Tuesday, when hopefully I can sort out the ferry across the Caspian. More horror stories on the World Wide Web about that trip, but I'll discover the truth for myself after I've experienced it.

I stayed for my last night in Georgia at a little 'hotel' in Lagodekhi. The Bio Yard is a collection of small wooden huts in a tranquil, shaded spot right at the entrance to the national park in the Caucasus Mountains, run by amazingly friendly English-speaking hosts and it's as cheap as chips. Billed as an eco-friendly destination, I shared a pleasant evening with some fellow British adventurers who sounded rather 'well-to-do' and were walking around interesting points in the foothills well off the beaten tourist path. The bill on departure was a very acceptable twenty Georgian lari (about £6) and the owner would take no payment for the very palatable jug of home-brewed wine I consumed the previous evening.

If you're travelling from Georgia to Azerbaijan, it really is perfect and only 3km away from the border.

The approach to the border itself was mildly amusing, with a sign in Georgia that says 'AZERBAIJAN BORDER AHEAD – GOOD LUCK'. A smile from the Georgian policeman and I crossed to the dark side.

8 AZERBAIJAN – THE LAND OF FIRE

Action Stations, Azerbaijan. With numerous police, army and customs officials buzzing around, my passport and international driving license, my registration document and visa were all scrutinised and whisked away in various directions while I was asked to unpack everything.

Sometime later, when I had undone one pannier after much deliberate messing around by me of making a big show of unfastening various bungees and removing bulky items from the back of the bike, I pronounced the contents of my luggage available for viewing. A quick shuffle through my medical kit and the customs guy got bored. The policeman asked if I had any religious books, had I been to Armenia and did I have a knife? After resisting the huge temptation to be my usual humorous self, I simply replied in the negative to all. After another round of mildly bored investigations into my collapsible spade and photos of me and the bike's registration plate, the little matter of $30 in the nice policeman's pocket for the documents I needed and a limited date for the bike to stay in the country and I was set free to engulf my senses in the wonders of northern Azerbaijan.

And therein lay a conundrum as, despite all the horror stories, bad news and warnings, it was actually a very nice place to be. The road from the border isn't the nicest bit of tarmac I've ever ridden on, but the scenery went from lush, green wooded hills to flat, open, baked farmland as I travelled over bridges spanning wide, rocky, dry riverbeds where locals bathed in the shallow pools of waters that still lingered lazily in the summer heat.

With over 400km to Baku it wasn't all pleasant travel, but as the road winds its way along the foot of the hills heading east it passes through some wonderful places with wooded areas awash with shaded eateries advertising their wood-grilled meat by letting the smoky aroma waft into the road to entice the weary traveller. Later on vendors offered more fruit than you could throw a vegetarian at, with the biggest watermelons I have ever seen, for sale by the van load. How many melons can you sell in a day? Ask an Azerbaijani farmer! Nuts by the supermarket carrier bag full are offered to passing traffic by overenthusiastic youngsters darting in front of the traffic. My one tricky moment came as I rounded a sharp corner that had a large amount of loose gravel in the road, forcing me to run wide, until I realised there was nothing between me and a huge vertical drop down a cliff, my front wheel skidding to a halt only inches from certain doom!

The last 100km of the journey traverses an arid desert of rocky, rolling hills bisected by a new ribbon of bright blue/black tarmac in the otherwise sandy scene. But with a high 30°C temperature and a strong gusty side wind blowing for the duration, I spent all my concentration on simply staying on said tarmac rather than on the unfinished sides. Two other points highlighted this little part of the journey for me. I spoke to a few locals en route and all were smiling and friendly, asking where I was from and where I was going, lots of drivers waving and tooting appreciation as they passed. The second was that, despite other reported experiences, I managed to slip under the police radar. There are a lot of them, but my paranoia over police corruption and common bribery proved unfounded as I stayed well within speed limits. I saw a few speed camera guns being operated by non-uniformed personnel in parked unmarked BMWs, but no one took much notice of my little Kawasaki.

The first impressions of Baku are of a modern, busy city that is keen to impress, with a plethora of high-end motors rumbling through the seaside streets. The tall glass buildings and expensive hotels on the seafront shout that it's an obviously wealthy town in sharp contrast to the countryside farmers' Soviet Ladas and one-horsepower carts. It remains to be seen if the ferry lives up to the legend. The Caspian awaits.

Baku Blogging (read in a dour, gravelly American private detective voice, with a nod to numerous film noir characters) Baku, the windy city. Where a guy can get lost in his thoughts of escape over the shining sea.

The trick in this situation is there is no trick, no matter what the movies tell you. No rules, no secret mantra, no road map. It's not about how smart you are or how good you were; it is chaos and luck, and anyone who thinks differently is a fool. All you can do is hang on madly as long and hard as you can. Then you might just get that ticket for the ferry.

It does feel a bit like a game, one official saying one thing, another ticket office directing me to another location that I never found. An (expensive) phone call that explains there was a boat today, but it had no space for a motorcycle. But there will be tomorrow. Maybe. We'll see! I ring back tomorrow and revisit the ticket office. All the while, my vehicle permit expires in the morning. The local advice seems to be to park it at the port, effectively in no man's land, and leave it there. Not sure I'm overly happy with that. Next game move, please. I don't know how to get around the permit situation right now. I read there's a customs office in town that might be able to extend the date on the permit, but I haven't been able to find anyone who knows where it is.

Apart from the technical issues, I like the people here. In a cafe the proprietor fills my glass with a cool soft drink and when I'm not paying attention he returns to refill the half-empty glass from the bottle he left on the table. Modern, air-conditioned shopping malls with high profile brand names and a Lamborghini parked in the foyer have everything except, it seems, many customers. Bentley, Ferrari, Maserati, Prada, Versace, Gucci. You name it; they are here. New oil money, I guess, will filter down to the less well heeled in time. But time isn't on my side right now. Just need to find a boat and buy a one-way ticket outta Dodge. Plenty of those around too!

Baku continued – King's pawn to E4 and checkmate, Snookered behind the black and match point; they win, I lose. My only option on Tuesday has been to leave the bike parked in the customs area at the port because I am not allowed to ride it with the transit permit expired and it can't be extended. It will either be okay or it won't. Make or break point at the minute. If everything goes missing before I get back to it, my trip will be changed. I hope the officials are as official as they seem. I'm sure I'm not the first to go through this loop. In the meantime, I've got a hotel room and a phone number to call for news about the ferry departure. I've just got to sit tight and wait, making a nuisance of myself to Vika on the phone until she says yes. She's the dame with the game, and although I have the entry stake I don't know where the table is or which pack of cards we're playing with.

With the bike stuck there's no immediate concern now. My personal visa is valid till the end of the month and once the stars align I'll be gone. Getting to the Russian border by the time my visa starts shouldn't be an issue, I hope. And if time and distance prove to be more critical in Russia, there is always the chance of boarding the Trans-Siberian Railway for a few miles. Good news time, though, is that the wonderfully efficient South Koreans have allowed me to reserve the ferry from Vladivostok via their online booking system. At least I know when and where that boat sails.

The next day I get a positive answer from my morning phone call and I am directed to get myself to the ticket office ASAP except no one seems able to give me clear directions to where the ticket office is actually located. After chasing a wild goose all over town, I finally track down the mysterious Vika and I grasp the golden ticket. She says I should go straight to the port. So just after 2pm I get to Baku port, where the customs man tells me the ship is actually departing from Alat, about 70km south. As my bike has been parked (safely as it turns out) in the customs office, because the transit permit has expired, that might be a problem. Or not, it seems, as the nice customs inspection officer takes my seventy-two hour vehicle transit document, stamps it, signs it and writes a few words with tomorrow's date on it. "Good luck," he says with a smile and a firm handshake. My thanks are a confusion of what happens now and relief at some positive progress.

With no clear understanding of where I'm going, I take the coastal road out of Baku, figuring the port will be by the sea! Near the town of Alat, a sign to Baku International Trade Port looks right and is – I think. A policeman says, "Yes" – I think, – when I ask a one-word question of "Kazakhstan?" The one official on duty in the eight deserted passport control booths at a newly built gate with multiple empty lanes marked for trucks, cars and vans says, "Wait" – I think, So I settle in what shade I can find next to my bike propped on its side stand and my hat pulled low over my eyes. Just as I get vaguely comfortable, he calls me to his post marked as 'exit from the port only'. But hey, he's got a choice of any of them and no other customers for me to queue behind. A brief check of documents and with an uninterested wave of his hand I am pointed to what appears to be a customs office where a nice lady – I think – glances at my passport and shoos me away. That's it – I think?

I ride up the empty port road where a train is being shunted aboard. While I wait, a port worker in a hard hat directs me to an office where a nice lady – I think – takes 5 Azerbaijani manat (about £3) for something or other that provides me with a receipt and another ticket and I'm directed aboard the *Karabakh*.

9 THE *KARABAKH* – CROSSING THE CASPIAN

Wednesday 15th 4pm – on board the Azerbaijan-registered *Karabakh*. My bike lashed to the side of the deck alongside huge haulage trains and trucks, I'm taken onto the bridge, where I meet the captain and crew. A happy-go-lucky bunch, it seems, the captain making tea for the crew and sharing chocolates. Four cyclists also come on board: two English, John and Jen, heading for musical enlightenment in Indonesia, Italian Marco and Tifan, his French partner, heading for adventure on the Pamir Highway. By chance, the latter two I had asked if they knew where the ticket office was when our paths crossed earlier in the day as we all played the game of 'find Vika and her mobile ticket office'. They too had been given the 'opportunity' to travel to the port of Alat to catch the boat, but their journey necessitated a taxi ride with bicycles in the vehicle. Late in the evening and I'm now sharing my less than luxurious cabin with an Azerbaijani lorry driver. We departed somewhere after 11.30pm. Hard to say when exactly, as the day's exertions caught up with me and I woke in the night with the rumble of the engines throbbing through the ship. Even with earplugs in it would be impossible not to feel them, but my internal motion sensors told me we appeared to be stationary.

Thursday 16th 7.30am – I woke on Thursday morning

to find I was partly mistaken. We were indeed stationary, but far out to sea. Strangely, the *Karabakh* seems to shrug off the movement of the waves, sitting motionless at anchor, the wind and water unable to disturb its bulk. With the trains on board it seems there is enough weight to steady its movement. The Azerbaijani lorry driver was up and gone before I woke and I saw him at breakfast, where he welcomed me with a smile, a "Salam" and the offer of a seat at the table. We broke our fast sat with the four cyclists and a shared pot of coffee. We appear to not be in any rush to make progress today. So sitting in the 'lounge' listening to the unfamiliar daily routine of a working ship, I pass the time with a book and some music. There's only so much sea you can look at. One wave is not much different from any other after a while. A steady wind keeps the air fresh and it's time to relax as much as possible and wait. Food is available on this vessel and the jolly cook is more than happy to oblige with vegetable soup and pasta dishes. A small table for we few passengers and regular mealtimes provide a time to chat and share in the experience of the journey.

Thursday 16th 4.00pm – we have been stationary since I woke. The crew spent the day hosing the ship down and in the process giving my bike a wash under the runoff from the deck. I hope a salt water dousing doesn't cause it any problems as, by the time I realised, it was already as wet as it was going to get. I can only guess we will make further headway later today and presume we will stop in Baku perhaps to pick up further cargo. I don't understand any other reason we might be waiting offshore except for a berth to come available. Hard to judge distance, but land is on the portside horizon and in seven hours I doubt we got much further than the 70km back to Baku.

Thursday 16th 6.30pm – the engines have been run up to speed, their huge torque making the ship shudder as the levitation awakes. Maybe we will progress again today? Or not. At 7.00pm all is quiet again. Engine trouble? Or just the Azerbaijani way? After an evening meal of vegetable soup and a strangely tasty mushroom and meat dish there is time to watch the sunset over the Caspian, which sounds much more romantic than it actually is over this dirty bit of salt water. There is not much more to do but retire to my cabin and read some more.

Thursday 16th 10.30pm – it seems we have spent the day sheltering in the lea of a spit of land east of Baku from a strong northerly wind, which seems like an awfully good idea to me given the reported shallow draft of the freighters on this route and their known propensity for capsizing. It remains to be seen when we actually make a run for it across to Aktau.

Friday 17th 7.40pm – woken to the rumble of diesel engines and the anchor chain clanking the lump of metal at its end up from the seabed. Looks like we will be underway today. A cooler, cloudy morning. I was awake a few times in the night and a single pesky mosquito buzzed around my ear for a while. It won't be feeding on anyone's blood again. The luxury toilet is blocked and the less than pleasant bathroom is even less appealing this morning. My lorry driver shipmate seems to be sleeping in his truck, which is probably more comfortable. So it's time to face the day and watch the waves pass by as we cruise north-east.

Friday 17th 10.00am – well underway. Under cloudy

skies with a little rain and a brisk wind, the green Caspian making a valiant attempt to look more like the North Sea than the exotic eastern waters of travellers' imaginations, the *Karabakh* still failing to be troubled by the rolling waves as it ploughs its course north by nor'-east. I missed breakfast this morning by choice. A glug of fruit juice and a chocolate croissant from my own supplies was enough to start the day. With no physical exertion on my part, my appetite has lessened. There will be food later in the day if I'm hungry.

Friday 17th 01.00pm – lunch was a thin soup with barley and vegetables followed by chicken wings with potato and peppers. I must be getting bored. I'm writing about the menu! The Caspian has turned to a deeper blue and the ship now has more of a battle at its prow to part the rolling swell as we cross the widest part of the voyage to Aktau. The *Karabakh* seems to have come to some agreement with physics that a ship should at least ride the waves and appears to have begrudgingly admitted some leeway to nature.

Friday 17th 6.30pm – I passed the afternoon chatting with Marco, the Italian cyclist, as he explained his understanding of quantum physics. We lightheartedly discussed the belief in cosmic ordering and the expanded conscience enriched with the benefit of travel, after which I returned to my less substantial reading. Having walked both decks available several times there is nothing much more to do other than return to my book, listen to a little music and dress for dinner. Or maybe just turn up again in the same jeans and T-shirt I've been wearing for the last few days. Evening entertainment, a cabaret, a cocktail bar, on-board shopping: all of these are not available on board the good ship *Karabakh*. But, as she toils across the now grey waters, we are heading to my next destination. I think we should be there by Saturday and hopefully there will be little delay in getting into port. If that works out I still have just over two weeks to cross Kazakhstan to get to the Russian border. But here I go thinking too far ahead again.

Saturday 18th 7.30am – I woke after a good night's sleep to calm waters. The *Karabakh*, it seems, won its battle with the waves. Checking the GPS on my phone, we appear to be just off the coast of Kazakhstan. I guess we'll arrive in Aktau later this morning, assuming there is a berth available.

Saturday 18th 1.00pm – we have been anchored off the coast of Kazakhstan for just over an hour now. Aktau is off the starboard side, tantalisingly close and yet so far. We are waiting for the port authority to give clearance to enter. I read a lot of accounts of travellers waiting for days for that to happen. I hope I don't have to report something similar!

Saturday 18th 4.00pm – the ship is berthed in port. Passengers confined to cabin please.

7.00pm – customs, immigration and military on board. Passport returned. But still not been allowed to disembark.

8.00pm – please board bus to passport control. Didn't you just come on board to do that? Long story abbreviated, I got across the border at 10.00pm, ride to Aktau. First hotel I found, thanks, 6000 tenge? I can't begin to work out the currency conversion and I don't care, thanks; just need a shower. Dry land, Kazakhstan; it's all been too much today. Badly, badly, badly, badly need a shower and sleep.

10 KAZAKHSTAN – INTO THE GREAT WIDE OPEN

Well, the border entry was a mess of paperwork, stamps, signatures, officious officials, young military guys goofing around, playful and joking with each other with a ready smile until the commandant's arrival brought serious faces. Mongolian faces. Stern faces. Red tape and more rubber-stamping on reams of duplicated paper forms that needed counter-signatures and recording in a ledger before seemingly being entered into a computer. You get the picture! An Australian guy on a bike heading west was going through the same process. The cyclists managed to get through the technicalities more quickly with no vehicle to register, and I didn't see them again. A hotel at 6000 tenge (KZT) is about £20, with shower fittings that aren't, but the water is hot, the bed is comfortable and that's enough.

First impressions of Aktau aren't wonderful; it appear to be rows of post-Soviet housing. But there are signs of newer modern buildings and like most ports or borders I'm sure it won't be representative of the rest of the country. A MIG fighter reaches for the sky but is permanently tethered to the ground. As an art statement I'm not sure it's a very positive one. So plan for day one is to get out of town, assuming I can find fuel for the bike and myself on a Sunday, and head inland a way. Maybe that way I can lose the effect of the ship's movement that my head still seems to be experiencing. I left the hotel at somewhere around 10.30-ish in the morning, give or take an hour. It's Sunday, that much I do know. I hadn't noticed the time change last night. But then I didn't notice a lot by the time border patrol had fried my patience.

Day one in Kazakhstan consisted of finding a supermarket to stock up on food, understanding how the fuel stations work and getting out to town. The roads are rough: heavily worn tarmac giving way to dirt track and roads that are just tracks through the land at the side of what was once a road. I filled up the petrol tank with some local help. I have to pay first and fill up afterwards. Tricky when my Russian language learning stalled before I left home. Having carried spare fuel cans all the way across Europe, I didn't fill them up at the same time. An hour of fear later in the day on the ride to Beyneu, thinking I was going to be stranded in the middle of nowhere, taught me the valuable lesson of keeping that additional store of fuel topped up in a country that hasn't got a friendly petrol service station in every town or highway. Either the fuel station in Beyneu was out of calibration or I managed to squeeze in more than the capacity of my 19-litre petrol tank when I got there, literally running on fuel vapours. I need to rethink some of the routes and distances I can cover in a day.

Two nights in Beyneu at a comfy little hotel give me time to check the best routes that the bike can deal with and by lucky circumstance avoid a massive thunderstorm with enough rain to fill the deepest of craters in the roads. That would have been interesting! Advice from a fellow traveller suggested my planned direct route from Atyrau to Aktobe meant traversing an extremely difficult road that a fully equipped off-road bike would struggle to cope with. The recommended route means taking a 1000km diversion from Atyrau, north to Ulralsk before heading east again to reach Aktobe, but it will be far easier on me and my little Kawasaki.

So a ride to Atyrau was an easy 400+km on good roads and in relatively cool temperatures. I was expecting 40°C in the desert, but early in the day it was a comfortably low 20°C. The dry scenery is punctuated with herds of camels and horses, some of them tethered or hobbled with two front legs tied together, which indicates they belong to someone, but the herdsman must have a hell of a job finding them on the vast plains that disappear to the horizon.

Trains of more than seventy carriages cross these huge open spaces hauling goods past infrequent oil refineries to low-rise breeze-block housing in sparse towns, with little to show why someone would live there and what they would do for work, money or food. Kazaks still living the old ways out in the steppe.

Kazakhstan konundrums – I know I've talked about inner country contrasts before, but Kazakhstan is the biggest difference I've noticed so far. While Georgia and Turkey showed dramatic differences between rich and poor, haves and have-nots, Kazakhstan has all that and more. Seemingly wealthy and 'Western'-influenced major towns with every modern convenience. In Atyrau, iPod-equipped teens on roller blades, cyclists and joggers share the riverside with old fellas chewing the fat while they keep a sharp eye on their fishing line out in the Ural. Yet, only an hour's ride out of town, rough breeze-block buildings cower in the midday heat on the dusty, windblown steppe. Air-conditioning is THE luxury to have. And yet there are still teenagers with their noses buried in mobile phones wherever you are. It's a universal truth. The twenty-first st century reaches even the poorest areas when the youth of the world need to access Facebook.

A two-night stopover at the relatively luxurious Hotel Victoria in Atyrau gave me time to rationalise my luggage a little. I haven't used the water container I've carried across Europe, and other non-essential items have been given away or left for any potential scavenger. A wood-burning stove? I'll just light a fire. A folding spade? For what exactly? These things seemed worthwhile while I was planning. Now, out in the real world, I need to shed some weight and make life easier. "We carry our fears in our luggage" were words of wisdom I heard recently and it's true. Carrying everything I think I need is pointless. I either use it or it's not worth carrying. The bike is significantly easier to handle as a consequence.

Kazakhstan continues to be a land that opens your mind to new experiences. Wild, wide open spaces; vast, windswept plains; dry riverbeds and lakes baked dry by the sun. Camels and horses showing little interest in passing traffic even when they stand in the middle of the road trying to stare out an eighteen-wheeler truck. I give way to a camel every time on my little bike! Sandblown towns, oil-rich modern cities, poor Russian leftovers, new Japanese 4x4s and policemen with big hats. New tarmac, lots of big road building projects and roads that don't even come close to the noun; a dirt track would be a compliment to some. I'm sure there are areas on the moon that are easier to navigate. In the end it is a country struggling to drag itself into the present day and overthrow the image presented by one comedy actor. I like its spirit, its people are as hopeful and modern thinking as any other I have passed through.

Thursday's 500km ride north to Uralsk on the first leg of my 1000km diversion was a seemingly unending, straight road across flat, open scrubland. This north western side of Kazakhstan makes even Holland seem mountainous! Huge sweeping vistas to the horizon and beyond sight, populated by more camels, horses and remote low-rise towns baked to a dusty crisp. Solitary people waiting for a bus ride literally in the middle of nowhere. My mind working overtime as I reached for the never-ending horizon; I spent a while trying to figure out where someone like that had come from or was going, to be standing at the side of the road in the midday heat.

I met two bike riders on the way, the first while I was still in Atyrau. Two up on a Ukraine-registered BMW K1300, he was following his built-in satnav and heading direct to Aktobe. I offered him the advice I was given about the road and suggested that if a rider on a KTM Adventure had found it difficult, he might struggle on his continental cruiser. I don't know if he took my advice or decided to find out for himself. The second bike was again two up on a Russian-registered BMW F800. I pulled up as they were stopped at the side of the road. All was well, but it seemed the pillion was less than happy. A thumbs-down signal with the word Kazakhstan said it all. They were running for home and the nearby Russian border. They whizzed past me a little while later with a wave that I returned when I again passed them when they stopped a short while after. Not enough seat padding, I suspect.

I pre-booked a hotel in Uralsk, online from the comfort of the Hotel Victoria, simply because it saves spending ages finding somewhere and sorting out prices and such. In this case booking.com came up trumps and a four-star hotel at three-star prices provides a welcome touch of luxury on the trip. From Uralsk I will again start to head east and back 'on route'; with eleven days to go to the start of my Russian chapter, I've got time to take it easy and explore the areas I stop at and that's just fine by me.

If you have the fortunate misfortune to find yourself in Uralsk, make sure you find yourself a room at the Pushkin Hotel. Named after the famous Russian poet and playwright who stayed in the town while collecting historical material for his story *The Captain's Daughter*, it is the only gig in town worth being at. It felt slightly hedonistic to book a four-star hotel on this trip, but the modernity on offer is in stark contrast to the real world outside its front door. The main street of Uralsk is a blend of old colonial pre-communist Soviet buildings, a church from the sixteenth century and well-kept parkland alongside the ever-present mighty Ural. The river defines the town's history as it was an important trade stop for barge traffic plying trade between the Caspian Sea and the Ural Mountains for centuries. These days a dam keeps the river level artificially high as its dark waters brood under the intense summer heat. There is a sense of being closer to Russia than its Kazakh roots, with modern art memorials to the Red Army and the hotel that insulates you from it all with modern Western influences: fluent English- speaking staff, steak and chips on the menu and cold beer at the bar. That brief diversion from the way of life I have was very welcome. Not that it's difficult to be as nomadic as I am; it was just nice to find somewhere where it was easy to communicate.

Fast forward a few days and I've travelled the 500km from Uralsk to Aktobe. An immediately forgettable location. A simple hotel provided a day to prepare for the long ride to Kostanay. Making sure I was prepared this time. Fully fuelled up, jerrycans filled, water and food on board. A distance of 800km over roads that sometimes were and sometimes weren't. A testing day saw the scenery change from dry vistas that have characterised my journey through Kazakhstan so far to a far greener and consequently wetter area. A seemingly endless grass steppe that is populated by large numbers of huge birds of prey, a mass of floating feather and claw that after some internet investigation appears to include eagles, buzzards and harriers, eventually gave way to farm crops as far as the eye could see. The thought of preparing the ground or harvesting those crops boggles my mind! It must be a huge undertaking if your field is the size of an English county!

I posted a YouTube video of the many and varied road conditions; making progress was sometimes a slow and painstaking affair. Short areas of new tarmac were followed by a long section of road that had been levelled and covered with an oil preparation that sprayed me and the bike with sticky black goo that got baked on by the engine and the midday sun. Other parts of the journey were badly broken-up old tarmac with potholes that would swallow my bike whole. Dirt road that was okay in places, but almost demolished by heavy vehicles in others and roads where traffic had invented its own route alongside the original. Luckily, I'm travelling during the summer and the dirty roads are at least hard packed and just about navigable. Mix in winter rain and snow and this would be impossibly impassable.

I calculated, during my last stop, that I had a fuel range of somewhere near 350km in the petrol tank, plus another ten litres of fuel in the cans that would extend that by about 160km. So I planned to fill up as near to the 350km limit as I could. After leaving Aktobe, I only passed one fuel station and I had covered 300km. That was close enough to my estimate to fill up and it turned out to be a very good idea as the road disappeared shortly after, meaning my fuel consumption calculations went out of the window with the tarmac, to be followed by miles and kilometres of gravel, sand and packed dirt. It was a tough day's riding.

I arrived late on Monday evening in Kostanay, a town founded by pre-Soviet Russians in 1879 and named Nikolaevsk in honour of Tsar Nicholas II until the Red Army took control in 1918 and changed the city's name, executing the anti-communist Alexander Vasilyevich Kolchak and his army in 1920. A room in a little hotel provided a place to sleep for twelve hours following the trek to get here. I stayed two nights on the outskirts of the modern little town to rest and recover a little before again undertaking what turned out to be a mammoth trek to Astana.

The first 100km of this 700km journey was easy enough with good tarmac under the wheels, although the M36 was more like the B36! Northern Kazakhstan is about on the same latitude as northern England and under typically cloudy 12°C skies it was cool enough first to swap to my heavier (warmer) gloves and even to switch the heated grips on for the first time since the Alps. As the weather darkened, so the recurring theme of deteriorating roads returned as they went from older tarmac to my personal favourite of deep-potholed-badly-worn-out tarmac to tarmac that no longer fitted the description. With rain now falling, it was 'pot luck' to avoid the deepest holes. As if that wasn't challenging enough, the huge expanse of open flatland allowed me to see huge rain cells approaching as the clouds darkened still further. In places it wasn't possible to see the horizon as the curtains of water obliterated the view. Taking shelter from a particularly hefty downpour in a fetid bus stop, I met a guy who was hitchhiking from Tbilisi in Georgia to Mongolia, just for the fun of it! – and people think I'm adventurous!

Some 500km into the journey, the road arrived in both Kokshetau and the twenty-first century, with a three-lane motorway conducting me the remaining 200km, all the way to the city of Astana, that at first glance under black skies seemed more fitting as a Batman movie set than the glittering capital of Kazakhstan. Riding through continued torrential downpours, I kept a further weather eye on cars stopping at the roadside to purchase fruit goods from vendors, itinerant farm animals and wandering pedestrians, all on a 120kph motorway!

Astana became Kazakhstan's glitzy new capital in 1997 and the name translates from Kazak to mean Capital City. A twelfth-floor apartment in a complex of blue glass buildings is mine until the weekend. So with a few days to take in the sights and sounds of Capital City the next day dawned foggy as low cloud obscured any view from the window as I munched on slightly stale bread and Nutella for breakfast. My first stop will be a supermarket. Time for a nice home-cooked supper and maybe some bacon for breakfast. Life is easy!

Later in the day and a warm sun played its rainbow light trick through fountained gardens that line the route between the blue-glassed high-rise buildings towards the presidential palace. Multi-coloured statues of horses painted in the flags of the world's nations stood in line on the approach to a modern shopping centre. Astana is everything that the rest of Kazakhstan isn't and it's poorer for it. A Japanese architect's idea of modern city development that has misplaced what it means to be Kazakh. They have seen modern urban city developments and see it as an attainable dream, instead of staying true to Kazakhstan's roots. A facsimile of the West instead of an original.

My last night in Kazakhstan was spent in Semey, which from 1949 to 1989 was the site of Russia's nuclear test facility. Not a place to linger long! But a sunny Sunday stroll in the park doesn't reveal any of the substantial issues that might have been evident from the exposure to the fallout from 456 explosive tests.

Kazakhstan konclusions – so my Kazakhstan finale dawns and time to reflect on the experience. Kazakhstan is absolutely vast. Massive open plains. Huge desert scenes. Incredible seas of grass steppes that meet the cerulean sky at the distant horizon. Those more than anything will be my overriding memories of this country. Although I fear the state of some of the roads may well be a resonant memory.

There is a big road-building programme going on and in the next five to ten years Kazakhstan will have a viable road infrastructure, so in some respects I'm glad I've seen it now because, despite the attention-grabbing potholes and rippled, broken down and just plain horrible tarmac in places, it somehow fits into the tableau of the country. Lines on a map do not necessarily mean there is a physical road in this country.

Zebra crossings in the middle of nowhere I can only think are for the benefit of camels, but they don't seem to have understood the irony. Similarly, bus stops that can't possibly benefit any potential customer are placed miles from any occupied areas, and road junctions, where the road at the intersection just disappears into nothing 100 metres from the crossroads.

Everyone I've met has been genuinely pleased to see a tourist in their country. Lots of car drivers waving and tooting as they pass in either direction.

It can be a dusty, hot, dirty, frustrating travel experience. You could easily think of the negative things that are part of the daily reality in Kazakhstan. But I like to think it has been a positive time. While it's true there is not a lot to see in between destinations, that remoteness provides a stark contrast in the eyes of someone more used to a country that is ten times smaller in area with four times the population!

Two weeks to cross Kazakhstan was a viable timescale. Did I need the off-road tyres I had fitted back in Turkey? Probably not in reality. They were useful in places, but there is enough road to not warrant that capability. I now have three weeks to get to Vladivostok – Russia beckons.

11 RUSSIA – ZDRAVSTVUJTE!

Monday the 3rd of August brought my Russian visa into action. With my usual trepidation I approached the end of Kazakhstan, fearing the worst if my six-hour endurance test on entry was anything to go by. As it happened, the border guards were significantly less officious on exit. I was asked if I had any drugs (adrenaline does me fine, thanks) or guns and pointed in the direction of the passport control office. Less than twenty minutes later I was on course for the Russian entry, which was swift and courteous as the customs guy took a cursory glance at the contents of my panniers, and after my passport was stamped I was allowed into the embrace of Mother Russia. A stop to purchase insurance for the month was completed with minimal fuss and equally minimal cash. At 750 rubles it is less than £8 for the month – bargain! And Russia has proper roads to boot! It's like re-entering civilisation.

My first destination was Barnaul, where I took a two-night stopover to allow me to fettle the bike a little. A thorough clean-up of the drive chain to get off what seemed to be most of Kazakhstan stuck to it proved it was mostly still okay. I'm a bit concerned about the need to do an oil change, but that will have to wait. The worst part was a broken bracket on the exhaust that had allowed a worrying tyre/exhaust interface to occur; the rough roads in Kazakhstan had taken their toll. A little less of a problem than three Belgian guys had with one of their bikes. Koen was trying everything he knew to resolve the problem with Steve's bike, while Niko chain-smoked through the whole process of sorting out a way to overcome the issue of a worn-out shaft gear on one of their three Trans-Mongolian Express Beemers.

On Tuesday evening Stuart and Olly, whom I travelled with into Georgia, and Ian, whom I met in Tbilisi, arrived not only in the same town, but at the same hotel as our paths crossed again. A night out at a local bar owned by a wealthy Russian oligarch caricature, who seemed intent on impressing his European customers, was a celebration of making it this far on our respective journeys. Russia, it seems, is not some dark distant land with overpowering political rule. So far it is a modern, relaxed, civilised country with good shops, modern roads, plentiful goods on the shelves and twenty-first-century gadgetry. So put away the ideas of cabbage soup and cross the border in your mind. "Velcome to Russia, my friends."

Planning ahead for my route will, I hope, bring me to Irkutsk by the weekend, which will mean I am one third of the way along my mammoth Russian trek. Hopefully, I can take a little break around Lake Baikal before tackling the prodigious distance to Vladivostok.

Rushing through Russia – At the risk of invoking every Russian stereotype you have ever imagined. Most Russians appear to have a real affinity with vodka! But served ice cold I can understand why. As a single malt whisky lover, a cold shot of vodka is a disparate but agreeable experience. All the trees that weren't in Kazakhstan? – They are in Russia. Millions of them. Mile after kilometre(!) of endless roads with trees, just trees! Silver birch and conifers by the score. They surround you, choke off views, they are a vast featureless nowhere and they are alive!

The petrol stations have a system where you pay up front for what you think you will need. The invisible attendant switching the pump off after it reaches the amount you have pre-paid for, or collecting the change once you've filled up. Which is fine now I understand it. It was more than just a bit confusing when the first petrol station I stopped at had a woman behind a mirrored window talking through a speaker with a sliding slot to put the money in before she switched on the pump. With no eye contact on my side, communication was somewhat difficult!

By Friday I've had to push on a bit. With over 6000km to cover in three weeks I can't hang around. Consequently, I've not had much time for film or photos; stopping to catch 'that' shot puts an enormous dent in my average speed and covering 800km in one day means that is crucial. A one-night stop in a pleasant hotel in the seemingly grim city of Novosibirsk, where a monument to the heroes of the Russian Revolution was a mandatory school field trip during the Soviet years, was just a pause in my journey, and a long day's ride brought me into Krasnoyark after sunset. Arrival in the dark in a strange city is always fun! Seeing flashes of lightning illuminate the yellow smog hanging over Krasnoyark from its aluminium-producing factories was a dramatic introduction to that particular city. A place where political exiles were once banished is never going to be the most beautiful city in the world, never mind the most beautiful in Siberia, as author Anton Chekhov once described it.

Friday night was spent in my tent in woodland next to the continuous rumble of the Trans-Siberian Railway. Getting off the road and into the trees ensured I was out of sight of any passing vehicles, but the wood was too damp for me to be able to light a fire, and I retired early. However, it did put me within a day's travel of Irkutsk on Saturday, which is right on schedule. A 5am start ensured I covered the 650km distance easily, despite some long roadworks diversions that routed the not insubstantial traffic, including some hefty trucks, through dusty and rutted forest tracks before allowing us all back onto un-repaired roads. At some point in the day I seemed to enter a Russian version of Lincolnshire. Dense forests of trees gave way to rolling hills and farmland, with islands of trees amongst the sun-ripened golden cereal crops, the only difference to the English version seeming to be the huge acreage, with collective nouns of combine harvesters working together to reap the crop.

Irkutsk arrived at 52° N 104° E and 40°C! Russia had been pretty cool until then! I'm sure Irkutsk will be cool in ways that most of the Russian conurbations I have passed through so far could never be. After three long days of covering the kilometres, 800 on the first day and 1000 split over the next two days to get here, it's time to have a day off to explore this little piece of Russia and hopefully see more than the bits and pieces that I have only passed through along the way. So far I've seen trees, roads and trees – and some fairly messy big cities. I'm sure there's more to offer than that. Lake Baikal and (on to) Ulan-Ude on Monday will, I'm sure, be highlights.

Browsing market stalls and wandering the old streets of Irkutsk with nowhere in particular to go, Karl Marx Street led me down to the riverside, where I found a restaurant and managed to order food in Russian. My order was a little lost in translation as I somehow ordered half a roast pig and a litre of local beer for myself. The massive overeating that followed will keep me going for days!

After a two-night stay in a cheap but clean little back-street hostel, the departure from Irkutsk started badly as rain on the cobbled street and slippery old tram tracks conspired to put me down on the road just five minutes into the day's journey. That, I guess, went some way to setting my mood for the day, which matched the atmospherics. No serious damage; a bent handlebar will straighten and a bit of a knock on the knee will be a little stiff the day after, but I'll live on. Just annoyed at myself for what is really a rookie mistake. Crash bars on the bike and the body armour in my kit saved the day.

Baikal Blues – Blues as in Russia is difficult at times and today has been testing. No blue skies travelling from Irkutsk to Ulan-Ude, just grey cloud, cool temperatures and occasional rain. No blue water either, the great lake all but hidden from view by the endless trees. Russia has again become a road, lined with trees hiding anything that might be interesting, punctuated by mainly grim cities and paranoid petrol station cashiers. Is this all that Russia is? I'm just not feeling good about Russia right now. Initially, it was a pleasant change after Kazakhstan's trials but further east it's just grey, tree-lined and mostly uninteresting. The people I've met seem mostly the same: more interested in their mobile phone conversations than customer service. I know I don't speak the language but give me a break here! The language barrier is no different to being in any country. In the end different words for similar meanings is just a case of education, but when the alphabet is different it sometimes gets a bit cryptic, or should that be a bit Cyrillic? Sometimes it would be nice to have someone around to pick me up both metaphorically and, as it happens today, literally! It's just been a bad day, that's all; with a few repairs to sort out I'll take some time in Ulan-Ude before moving on.

Russian Revolution – no, not a history lesson, but a revolution in my thinking. Monday was a day that started badly and didn't improve as I travelled. Arriving in Ulan-Ude late in the day and finding a comfortable hotel eased me into the evening with a chicken kiev and a glass of beer to settle my mind and rest an aching body. After a good night's sleep, a sunny morning made light of the previous day's depressions.

I managed to straighten out the bent handlebars with the help of a local chap who wandered over to see what I was up to in the car park of the hotel. Using a woodwork lathe in his apartment basement as a clamp, it was sorted with minimal fuss. I also sorted out the overdue oil change and the bike was once again fit to travel.

An afternoon stroll to the nearby town square brought me to the destination of the Mongol rally, where cars were expected to arrive over the next few days, under the watchful eyes of the 7.7-metre-high, forty-two ton Lenin's head! The rally entrants are only allowed to drive small, cheap cars more suitable to city commuting than cross-continent rallying. There is no defined route; it is up to the drivers to decide the best way to make it to the destination. It is more mad adventure than competition rally, but the simple rules ensure that there is not much point cheating! I'm not even sure there is an actual winner. Just getting there qualifies as success.

After a couple of days resting my bruised hip and knee, I continued east from Ulan-Ude, my departure marked by a morning smog for which I failed to identify the reason. It was almost like a dense smoke clinging to the ground in fear of being dispersed by a breeze. Heading for Chita, the scenery got decidedly Siberian! Luckily, it's still too early for snow (I think), but with a chill wind and occasional rain some of the trees appear to be already shedding leaves as autumn colours spread through the branches. The wet road made a section of roadworks a sticky area to navigate across as sand, gravel and a deeply potholed loose surface coagulated to mire progress. But, with a determination to not repeat Monday's mishap, I made it through to the formally restricted military city of Chita, the outskirts of the city populated with huge concrete bunkers, presumably a remnant of the Cold War.

A hotel that at first glance appeared to be a small-town three-storey building, fronted what could easily have been a Russian villain's twelve-storey lair from a James Bond movie, with posters in the lifts for a basement strip club and uniformed soldiers stood in the corridor. It proved to be a comfortable base, although no one on the hotel staff spoke English. My basic Russian and a little universal sign language meant we managed to communicate with ready smiles. The next day Chita looked less imposing bathed in warm sunshine. I eventually found a supermarket, harder than it sounds when the entrance is a simple double-glazed UPVC door with very little in the way of signage to give a clue to the interior. With my supplies restocked with tinned meats and fresh fruit and vegetables in preparation for the 2000km trip to the next port of call at Khabarovsk, there was not much to do except sit in the main square under the obligatory statue of Lenin and watch the world go by under the watchful eye of the many numerous military helicopters that passed overhead.

More news on the future arrived by email from the shipping agent in Korea. I am having to plan ahead a little as I need to have some arrangements in place in time for my arrival in Vladivostok to catch the ferry to DongHae in South Korea. Before all that, there is the little task of crossing what became known as the Zilov Gap. A group of blokes who tackled a round-the-world journey that they called MONDO ENDURO on Yamaha XT350s in 1996 were brought to a muddy halt in that area, and they coined the name for the region that only the Trans-Siberian Railway crossed at the time. Ewan McGregor and Charlie Boorman's *Long Way Round* TV adventure in 2004 avoided it altogether, but these days it is the route of the M58 Chita Khabarovsk highway. Thanks, Mr Putin, for demanding a road be built between Moscow and Vladivostok!

Leaving Chita with a sense of trepidation at what to expect over the next couple of days, I was stopped at a police checkpoint. My first real interaction with the Russian police, but "Ya ne govoryu pah Rooski" ("I don't speak Russian") seemed to satisfy his curiosity after he inspected my international driving licence and registration documents.

With almost no civilisation after Chita apart from truck stops, remote fuel stations and the ever-present Trans-Siberian Railway, the 'super' highway to Vladivostok doesn't include the small towns en route and consequently appears to have brought little benefit to those communities who still rely on the railway to make it through, whatever the season.

Chilled early mornings are definitely autumnal this deep into Siberia. With long, dark winters, summer is a brief fluctuation in our imagined vision of frozen permafrost, but the days warm up considerably and the squadrons of mosquitoes still believe it is summer, with vicious attacks on any single patch of exposed flesh.

I passed a few bikes going west. A single bike late in the day on Saturday when I was slowing in places to look for a campsite. The first was a Honda 650 Transalp, I think, with a yellow registration plate, but he didn't slow as he passed. I hope he found as good a campsite as I did. Then early on Sunday, a group of eight bikes approached, all the riders waving enthusiastically as they passed. Led by a rider on a BMW GS adventure and followed up by a similar bike, it looked like an organised trip.

Two nights' wild camping provided the rest in between covering the distances required to cross this section of the journey. The first night in a disused quarry provided a sandy bed, and a small fire kept the worst of the insects at bay for a while. I was up at first light, keen to make

112

the most of the daylight and get some distance under the wheels. Stopping to refill the petrol tank at a truck stop 75km later showed that even out here expensive petrol is a global rule when it's out of town. It might be more expensive than it is in towns, but with a price that is the equivalent of £0.41 a litre I'm not complaining. Despite it only being 92 RON available at the pump, my bike at least seems to cope okay on the low-octane fuel, which is just as well as that's all it is getting.

By lunchtime the temperature was back up to above 30°C and using my new-found navigation app on my phone meant I had an idea of the distances between fuel stops, making life a lot easier as I was no longer riding into the unknown for distances and the fuel I need. Out here in the wilds of Siberia the fuel stations are remote. The cashiers sit behind mirrored and barred windows and as with everywhere in Russia it is normal to pay up front before the pump gets switched on. I guess there are or have been lots of issues with fuel theft and possibly violence towards the fuel vendors; a friendly smile is not something you find while filling up.

Late in the day I sheltered under a bridge waiting for a torrential downpour to pass by, but, as the river beside me swelled and water crashed down around me as runoff from the road above, it seemed appropriate to get moving. Looking ahead, the dark clouds rolled on as far as I could see, but only thirty minutes later the land opened out from forest and woodland to farmland and the sun returned from behind the clouds, putting me and my bike on a fast-dry cycle as we rode along drying tarmac.

The bike has been overheating again today. I hope it is a symptom of the combination of ready-mixed road surfaces congealing on the radiator. I have stopped a few times to let it cool, but with no easy way of cleaning the fins of the radiator it's just a case of taking it easy. If I push on, the engine temperature warning light comes on, but if I ride steady then it seems to be okay. It could be a problem with a temperature sensor or it could be the radiator or even the low octane fuel, but I'm worried it might be something worse. I just have to keep looking after my little Kawasaki; it's me and it out here. I have to rely on us both making it back to some sort of civilisation. I do talk to it as I ride along. I know it's just a machine, but a rider develops an affinity with a bike in my experience. I've never gone so far as to call it 'her' or give it a name. I'm not that weird! But it's my travel companion, my lifeline and means of reaching my next destination. The alternative is a very long walk.

The second night in small woodland just off the road was equally peaceful but without the benefit of dry wood to get a fire going, but by then I had lost any idea of the time zone so was content to sleep when it got dark and move on when it got light. I was, however, woken up that night by what sounded like a large animal snuffling around the tent. I laid awake in the pitch black of night wondering if I should make a noise to scare it off or stay quiet. Thinking I would be awake all night wondering, I turned over and it was suddenly daylight; I had gone straight back to sleep. Some large footprints around the tent suggested to me I was visited by a bear, but it obviously found nothing of interest and moved on.

The scenery varied from vast swathes of deciduous woodland to marshland and coniferous forest. Valleys and hills and rivers too numerous to count. Crossing this land prior to the road must have been impossible, just as the Mondo Enduro guys endured in the 1990s, taking to the ever-reliable railway in the end. Just to try to put it all in perspective for anyone in the UK, it's like travelling from Land's End in Cornwall to John O'Groats in Scotland, then turning around and riding back to the English border. All without passing through any towns or villages. Just a vast wilderness that used to separate the Far East of Russia from the rest of this huge country.

Zilov Gap. Bridged! – well, the comparatively easy modern day route from Chita to Khabarovsk is nothing compared to the pre-road days. Prior to the road opening in 2004, making progress was measured in metres not kilometres. Hundreds of them at a time in my case! Khabarovsk, at the end of a long 2100km ride, is something of an oasis. A modern city named after a Russian adventurer who explored the region on the banks of the wide confluence of the Amur and Ussuri Rivers and only 30km from the border with China, which claimed the area as its own until the mid-1800s. Like everywhere else in modern Russia, Western brand names are on the high street and teenagers wander around with iPhones and trendy headphones. This far east, the locals are more likely to speak Japanese than English as a second language and almost all the vehicles in town are imported right-hand-drive motors from Japan. It feels strangely European despite being about as far as it's possible to be from that Western influence. With a beach on the river and pleasure boats cruising the waters, it has a coastal ambience as well, although I'm not so sure about the quality of the waters!

Now I'm in Khabarovsk I intend to take a little break from travel and enjoy a few days off. I don't have to be in Vladivostok until next week to catch the pre-booked ferry, so I can take a bit of time do a little bike maintenance and catch my breath prior to the final push to Vladivostok, which makes it sound more like a route march than a travelogue, but in places it has felt like crossing half the planet in one country! The seaside feeling of Khabarovsk continues with fast food joints on the riverside beachfront selling the American dream; well, a burger, fries and a Coke at least. While more traditional fare is available in town alongside another American dream in the shape of a Harley-Davidson branded bar, as an Englishman abroad I remain unconvinced as to the benefits of global Americanisation. The traditional kvas made from fermented bread is an infinitely more palatable experience than the iconic sugary black stuff and amusingly branded in some places as Nikola (or No Cola), despite the strange thought of making pop from bread and it being sold from barrels in the street, although the chemical ingredients of Cola probably don't bear thinking about either.

There are lots of Chinese tourists experiencing a Western consumerism-style vacation in far-eastern Russia, with Japanese products for sale, the united colours of branded clothing, and like everywhere else in the world the Union Jack is a symbol of cool. It's a strange world we live in, where adventurous travellers head east to experience the exotic and often find an imitation of the West. Global brands seem intent on homogenising the whole world. Despite all that, I like Khabarovsk; it is a comfortable place to be. It has the sense of being far away and yet somehow familiar, with trees and vegetation very similar to northern Europe and a summer climate not dissimilar to what we think a summer should be in the UK, without the rain! Sitting in the warm afternoon sunshine in one of the many neat parks with people promenading, rollerblading or cycling past, couples with youngsters, the gentle tumble of a fountain and the scent of freshly mown grass, it's hard to picture a frigid Siberian winter, or in fact the insect-infested harshness of a Siberian summer just a few miles north, but after weeks of exploring my own limits of endurance it is a pleasant experience.

I still don't have a definite plan for Korea, and shipping out of there has not yet been confirmed. One thing I am certain of is that I will travel without the bike for a while after Korea while it gets transported down under, much like the rest of the population (sorry, Australia!) So, with the world available to me at the flash of a credit card and a UK passport, I will have some time to take a more usual form of holiday travel to any place that will have me.

Setting off from my accommodation in the central park, my day started badly as heavy rain accompanied me. A fuel stop went wrong when I didn't pay for enough to fill up the tank, and the cashier refused to switch the pump on again even when I offered more rubles. The road deteriorated quickly and long distances of roadworks meant the road was non-existent, having simply been ripped up by diggers, leaving a wet mix of sand, gravel, diesel and potholes that inevitably undid the clean-up job I did on the radiator back in Khabarovsk.

My bike has taken a bit of a beating of late. Since the 'off' in Irkutsk it has been through tougher times than at any other point on the journey. While Kazakhstan's roads were rough, they were dry. Russia's roadworks, which involve simply removing worn-out tarmac, back to the rough base, are very similar to the Kazakh way, but the climate isn't. The chain has been through a grinding paste mix. It's becoming a bit of a regular theme, but it's time for a bit more maintenance. The tyres have just about had enough, and riding into Vladivostok in a rainstorm did little for my confidence. A local rider on KTM pulled up alongside as I searched for the right road into Vladivostok and stopped for a brief chat, seemingly oblivious to the pouring rain. It's the little things that pick me up when I'm feeling a bit low. Just like the German I briefly met back in Turkey, the enthusiastic greeting lifted my spirits. If bikers are guardian angels I've met my fair share on this trip.

Destination Vladivostok – I'm here! I have ridden my little Kawasaki from Merry Olde England to the far-eastern Russian port of Vladivostok! That fact on its own is amazing to me. To have ridden across blazing hot desert, dry grasslands, wet woodland and lush forests, over snowy mountains and through green valleys. To arrive here feels like a massive achievement. My 'targets', assuming I ever had any, included getting this far. To cross those huge distances, overland, just me and my bike. I celebrated with a local cabbage salad and a bottle of kvas! A room on the outskirts of town has a supermarket across the road and a jet-ski garage right next door, which is handy. Free use of a power washer will make things a little cleaner

Ready to go

Crossing the Alps

Italy and a view from San Gimignano

Italy and the view over Firenze

Getting tyres fitted in the bikeshop in Turkey

Kazakhstan desert skull

Russian memorial of the Moscow to Vladivostok roadn

Russia, crossing the Zilov Gap road to Khabarovsk

Russia, the *Eastern Dream* in Vladivostok

Arrival in Korea

Korean temple at Gyeongju

Great Barrier Reef snorkling

Australia at Phillip Island

South Australia

Australia starting the Great Ocean Road

Camping and one of the many option for the tarp extension

New Zealand, views near Queenstown

Visit to Hobbiton

On Route 66

Journey's End

for the bike to start with while I once again spend time on maintenance. The ferry operator's office was closed on Sunday, but at least I know where it is and I will be there on Monday morning to be ahead of the game for the ferry departure on Wednesday. In the meantime, I have had chance to swap the front tyre on the bike with a little help from my friends at jetski-club.ru who were more than happy to lend me a hand with workshop facilities right next door to my accommodation. Especially handy when the owner is a devoted petrolhead with his 250cc two-stroke Honda powered cart and various ongoing projects. He was more than a little interested in my bike and how I got here. He appears to have lots going on with jet-ski repairs, car bodywork (lots of work there with the standard of Russian driving) and what looks like two brand-new Subarus direct from Japan in the compound.

Vladivostok sits in at the end of the Muravyov-Amursky Peninsula in a hilly cove surrounding the Golden Horn Bay where the Russian pacific fleet sits at anchor. With a modern suspension bridge spanning the water, it has everything a modern waterfront city needs. It still feels slightly strange to stand taking photos of Russian warships and looking at World War Two memorials, when for years of my youth it was somewhere impossible to think that I would ever visit or had any desire to. This huge Russian bear hidden behind an 'Iron Curtain' in a dark, frozen corner of the globe: the subject of many Western-biased news stories, the site of secret Soviet and American nuclear agreements and usually home to the villains of fictional spy stories.

Tickets, Tariffs and Typhoons – The reported

paperwork difficulties were cast aside by the efficient expertise of Yuri and Svetlana at Links Ltd – contact them before anyone else, including the ferry company, if you need to ship out from Vladivostok, as they made the whole process simple. Just a case of waiting for each document to be completed and paying the necessary when required. With all the paperwork done, tickets purchased, customs fees paid and bike delivered to the customs dock, the DBS line *Eastern Dream* sits tied to the dock waiting to be loaded and we will be ready to go. Except maybe not: as Typhoon Gori sweeps through the South China Sea it appears there may be a delay. Not that it's an issue for me; my visa is still valid and I have time on my side in Korea. Sat dockside, the Panama-registered *Eastern Dream* was not the ocean-going liner I expected, but more a coastal cruiser. Given the reported ferocity of Typhoon Goni, I was happy to sit it out in Vladivostok. So, with everything prepared, I just have to wait and see what nature gets up to over the next twenty-four hours, which will determine if we depart on schedule. Time and tide (and typhoons) wait for no man!

Storm hits Vladivostok – The news on Wednesday morning told of little hope of Typhoon Goni weakening its hold on the South China Sea, and the shipping agent confirmed there would be no departure today. So as the rain increased to a steady downpour over Vladivostok I sorted out a room for the night and I have an extra day in town. My bike, it appears, is already aboard as it's gone from the customs dock along with a few other Korean-registered bikes. Well, at least one of us is on the ship; it's also one of us dry. As the steady downpour turned into a torrent, any sight of the sea disappeared in a curtain of rain as strong winds swept through the waterfront streets driving people to seek shelter. A comfortable apartment in the town centre is my own overnight shelter from the storm.

Thursday morning dawns calm but overcast; as I walk to the port there is blue sky on the horizon, which I hope bodes well. Waiting at the port, I seem to have become something of a celebrity as the Korean and Japanese tourists marvel at my height. Regular group photos ensue. I'm tall for Europe but hugely so in the Far East! Aboard the *Eastern Dream*, everything has changed. The sense of modernity is immediate. Duty free shops, café, bar and restaurant provide everything a passenger might need. Korea provides the currency, the traditions and the language. A small gathering around a stove cooks what appear to be small omelettes in a tiny pan. Although the ship has all modern conveniences, some of the cabins are simple mats on the floor. As we clear the islands around Vladivostok the skies clear of grey clouds and a relatively calm sea welcomes the *Eastern Dream*. I share an eight-berth cabin with one other passenger, and after a very comfortable sleep the morning dawns bright and clear, with calm seas and soon after, the faint blue haze of distant land on the horizon. Approaching a country by sea is something countless travellers have experienced over the centuries, but is denied to passengers in a modern world of air travel. From that glimmer of blue a landscape emerges, and then buildings, until the introduction is complete as the ship enters port.

Welcome to a whole new experience that is South Korea!

12 SOUTH KOREAN KARMA

Sat in a garden with the constant electric razor chirp of insects, next to a green pool teaming with leaping fish, it is easy to find the inner peace that the Buddhist temple over the stone bridge will preach. It is a place of quiet contemplation and somewhere to consider a sense of achievement in the distance I have covered so far, while a morning mist over the mountain backdrop adds to the scene. Intense incense burns under paper lanterns watched over by golden idols where peace and tranquillity are expected. An air of holiness is inescapable as reverent devotees offer their prayers to the symbol of light.

Arrival at the port was easy and fuss free. The insurance was expensive, though, at $331 USD. A sticker on the screen gives anyone who might be interested the details of the bike and the fact that it is legal. At least that's what they tell me. I can't read Korean! Travelling south, I initially got onto the equivalent of a motorway by mistake, but on the slip road entrance I noticed a sign with a motorcycle outline and a red cross through it, but it was too late; I'm already on it. A few kilometres further on, a policeman stood in the central reservation points his baton at me and crosses his arms in front of himself, indicating I shouldn't be there. I didn't want to be anyway and exited at the first junction I got to. Talking to a couple of bike riders later, it seems bikes are not allowed on any motorway in South Korea. Something about keeping up with the traffic! Really?

I was supposed to be meeting up with my brother here, but that hasn't happened. I rerouted my plans to match his move to South Korea, but he's still in Vietnam and won't be making the trip while I'm here. It was initially the primary reason for making this whole trip happen, after heart surgery. The plan developed into something more than that and now the doing has overtaken the thinking.

South Korea is a heady mix of modern and tradition. High technology, advanced electronics and an ancient history sit side by side. The culture is very different to my usual experience. The language is indecipherable to my European ears. Road signs unfathomable, and yet it seems relaxed and easy to manage. I don't expect to see the road ahead torn back to its stony base layer, and the supermarkets are stocked with everything I need. A lunch of rice and vegetables eases me through the afternoon, and not having to cover vast distances relaxes my senses even more. It's time to kick back and immerse myself in this exotic land.

Green Hills of Gyeongjo – With a few days to fill and various sites and attractions to visit, the week was entertaining and relaxing. Cool wooded hillsides with shaded walks, cafés and countryside parks. I've ridden my bike just for pleasure with no definite destination and no long distances to cover. Finding winding, little-used hill passes that have been bypassed by new straight freeways, along riversides and dams. It's a green place to explore; with few cars using these less direct routes, the roads are not busy and places to stop and admire the view are uncrowded. The crowds seem to gather at tourist hotspots, playgrounds, shopping centres and the like. There are lots of cyclists in the hills and campers at the beach, hybrid cars and wind turbines. Modern life, green countryside and warm days. A little meal at a local café is my birthday celebration of another year's anniversary, followed by a glass of my favourite Scotch whisky that was a parting gift that I have carried all the way from home as a departure gift, and a small cake from the supermarket in town.

After getting some fresh air and a bit of exercise walking through some of the woodland paths I will move south after the weekend to Busan, a fairly big city but somewhere I need to get to know a bit as I think my bike will be shipped from there later in the month. It will be a shame to leave the countryside I've stayed in recently, but there will be time later to look further at some more natural scenery once I have a better idea of time and place of packing my bike into the hold of a ship.

Buzzing around Busan – Busan is another big city, another mix of tall buildings and crowded streets. Not my idea of a good time but it fills my needs at the moment as I seek out transportation down under without resorting to stealing a penny bun! It's a cool place temperature-wise at a comfortable 20°C and there's lots of American influences, with coffee shops on every street and 7-11 stores on every corner. But as the Americans continue their mutual defence treaty in South Korea that has been in place since World War Two, I guess it's only to be expected. The centre of the part of town I'm in has a plethora of shopping, with everything available in all the well-known shopping chains and lots of others that are unknown to me, although that doesn't mean much, given my love of shopping. Food places of every flavour from the ubiquitous burger bars to seafood and traditional noodle and rice restaurants. A pan pizza is literally that, with a pancake-thin base served in a shallow pan! Unfortunately, air-tight sewer covers are not part of the street furniture and the waft of noodles, spiced meats and rice being prepared by street vendors is often accompanied by a less enticing aroma. A famous beach in town is less attractive than the less-hyped beach just outside the stylish busiest area. But there are large areas of wooded hillside visible from almost anywhere in the city. I'll make some time in the week to see if they are navigable on foot.

I found a small custom bike shop in the town. The owner builds café racer street bikes and race track-style Harley-Davidsons. He is trying to source a pair of tyres for me, but if not I'm comfortable that the last of the rear tyre will last for my time in Korea.

I'm struggling with the language. So far on the way I've made sometimes valiant, if often vain efforts to speak at least a few words when conversing with the locals, but Korean will just not stick in my head as I try to wrap my tongue around the strange mix of consonants and vowels in odd orders. I managed better with Russian and that's saying something!

Busan is somewhere that is easy to get on with, but would become tiresome, at least for me, if I were here for a length of time. I need more of a sense of space than is available, just like my time in any urban space I have stayed in along the way. Fewer people and more open skies work for me. In the meantime, I'll indulge myself in the modernity and avoid the crush of traffic, the mass of people and the scooters, using the pedestrian crossings where I can.

Inner city planning – Time to move, too long in one place has not been a good thing on this journey and too long in the urban sprawl of Busan is another of those times. I feel the need to get outta town and find some peace and quiet again. Finding space is not an easy thing to do. South Korea is a relatively small and quite heavily populated country. After the vast expanses of Kazakhstan and Russia I'm not sure I will ever look at travel across country in the same way again. At the time of writing there is still no news of shipping and while it's not a big issue right now I will feel more settled once I know when the next move will happen.

A few days later and there is some news. The bike will be shipped from Korea to Singapore and on to Australia in early October and, hopefully, it will be a relatively simple process, although I don't yet know the estimated delivery date. I then have to decide my own destination to fit around that schedule. So it's time to choose where to go while the bike is crated and transported. Once I deliver the bike to the shipping agent, I'll be in a whole new world without my own personal transport for the first time. I've never enjoyed public transport particularly, but trains and planes (without the automobiles) will be my means of getting about. So I'll look for somewhere that doesn't involve lots of travelling from an airport. Somewhere warm and less crowded, with a beach. Somewhere that won't cost a fortune. With all of South East Asia to choose from, that should be relatively easy. Maybe!

Some thoughts on Korea – Seasons: days are cooler at this time of year in South Korea. The sweltering heat of summer has passed over to more southern latitudes as the seasons turn, which is fine by me as I head west from Busan to explore a little before I return to surrender my two-wheeled freedom to a shipping agent with a wooden box.

More sights: maybe I've got a little blasé about seeing so many new things along the way but I feel like I've been in Korea long enough now. Yes, it's another river, another mountain, more strange towns and more unknown destinations; fresh perception, please. In other words, it is time to move on to the next country please.

Chatter: a chance meeting with a native English speaker (albeit an American one) is a chance to chat (probably too much) without seeing the lack of understanding in the victim's eyes. It's a strange thing to not have had a conversation for what seems like an age.

Country bumpkin: out of the big city, the pace of life is fractionally less frantic. As I've discovered along the way, I'm even more of a country boy than even I thought I was.

Korean cars: is that a Kia or a BMW? A Hyundai or a Mercedes? Was that a Maserati? Aston Martin? No, a Hyundai genesis. Korean cars have come a long way since the Daewoo Matiz. While they're not blatant copies, the styling cues catch me out. Just thought I'd mention it as my mind wandered during a traffic-heavy time.

Island dreaming: still facing indecision about where to aim for. I think my bike will be in Australia quicker than I anticipated as the shipping won't take as long as I thought. It can sit and wait for me for a while. It's not going anywhere without me. I'm a little concerned about being stuck in one place without transport and having to spend money on a holiday, although I can live pretty cheaply. Guess I need to download some good books and find a shady spot on a beach.

Time and relative dimensions in space – 'Travel broadens the mind' I must have heard that phrase an infinite number of times in my life. My parents exposed me to the joys of being abroad from the age of eleven. Living the good life in the Middle East in the early 1970s. I remember, though, that although money wasn't short in the family; we always travelled home to the UK for holidays. I don't know why. Hey, I was just a kid along for the ride.

The point is that despite the mind-expanding attributes of travel, we never forget who we are or where we're from. Even if that is the raison d'etre of your journey (it isn't mine). Fifty-two years of programming to look right first to cross the road isn't overridden easily.

I'm fairly used to being an 'odd one out' as well. Ever since I grew tall relative to most, people in the street seem to have thought I was blind and deaf to points or loud whispers. But in Korea I really am an odd, tall European in a population of Asian faces.

Korea is a confusion of culture for me and I don't mean that in a bad way. It has obvious American influences, with 7-11 shops and coffee bars. The golden arches don't appear to have pissed on everyone's burgers yet, though. It is a multitude of mediocre motels and a yen for modern tech. It's difficult to spot if the cars are Korean or European, which is a game in itself. Most signs and shops have English translations alongside the native language. I can't imagine the UK having non-English signs for the benefit of other cultures unless it's a benefits document from Sheffield Council.

If I was to choose to seek a life outside of my country of birth, I do know my choice wouldn't be here in much the same way it wouldn't be some southern Spanish resort with English breakfast on the menu. There is a balance between familiarity and being out of step. Modern Korea has everything someone might need, but it doesn't have enough space for me.

With time to spend, I seek peace in shaded gardens and woodlands, away from the manic race of life in the big cities. Nature gets squeezed in our ever-expanding population of the planet. When I thought I was absolutely in the middle of nowhere in Kazakhstan there was inevitably someone waiting for a bus. So in a small country like Korea it's easy to feel hemmed in.

Next week I venture back to Busan for my bike's appointment with a box. In lots of ways I'm looking forward to 'moving on', the phrase that has become synonymous with my journey and one I haven't put into practice for a few weeks now. Therein lies the root of my thoughts, I think. It's been an education but I don't feel the need for further study. A beach and some time to clear the interference from my head will cleanse my senses.

Having re-read that, it sounds like I'm overly unimpressed, which I'm not, if you follow my double negative. There are a lot of good things I have seen here. I have had similar feelings in almost every large city I have passed through. It's a sense of disappointment at human society. Homeless people sleeping in the station. The race to have everything now. Convenience food and a throwaway society. Cigarettes outside and forget your insides. Less personal space and build upwards. What's really important? I think that has to be a personal choice. Switch off your computer and explore the world. It has a lot more to offer than some virtual reality or toeing the corporate line.

Everyone has had a holiday they remember, a place where real life is set aside. The daily pressure of work parked for a while. But really, why can't life be like that? I'll tell you why… it's because you've got caught up in what you think is important. A new car, the latest phone, providing your kids with every modern need, having new clothes or the latest shoes, making your house as nice as your neighbour's and filling it with cinema-sized TVs. It's all frivolous.

As I look around, 99% of people are using mobile devices. Ironically, so am I; I'm not ignorant to my own failings on this score. Drivers are impatient because someone paused at a red traffic light. There's no time for each other anymore. No time for thought or accepting others' choices. While I'm not ready to live a hermit's life in a cave, my travel-expanded mind has yet to come to terms with a newer understanding of what makes me tick. Apart from my mechanical heart valve.

Moving on – well, that's that. After a week out of town offline from the connected world, I've re-entered the twenty first century. The bike is in a wooden crate; the shipping has cost $1450 USD and it will soon be on its way by sea to antipodean shores. Guess I had better be there to meet it!

In the meantime, I've got time to spend travelling to exotic shores for a little R&R. So an island off the coast of Thailand beckons for the coming weeks.

South Korea is a heady, sometimes difficult, mix of traditional and modern. It is very unlike my own and probably most people's preconceptions. Dog isn't on the menu of every restaurant, and rickshaws don't fill the narrow streets. Instead, wide, well-surfaced modern roads are populated with twenty-first century cars, and, as I've already talked about, burger bars and Western food are easily and readily available. Outside the crowded towns the countryside is lush and hilly, and beaches are good, where you can find space away from fishing villages.

But now I'm on my way. I've avoided air travel on this trip so far, but it's not very realistic to travel this leg by ship, so, airline ticket in hand, I'm about to board a big silver bird and take to the sky. Koh Samui, an island in the bay of Thailand, is my destination. Soft white sand, crystal-clear waters and a beachfront apartment will be home for a couple of weeks before I get myself to Darwin to collect my bike. I expect vistas of palm trees and sunsets over the beach. It's a dirty job...

13 KOH SAMUI – DESERT ISLAND DREAMIN'

Arriving after sunset, stepping off the narrow-bodied short-haul jet brought the familiar sensory shock of humidity. None of the gentle introductions of arriving by sea. Easing into a new country. Travel by air holds no such pleasantries. Bam! There you go. Get on with it. A suitably rustic airport building is approached via an open bus, but luckily my single 'travelling light' bag completed the same journey as me and a £2 taxi ride delivers me to a welcome air-conditioned room at the north of the island.

Welcome then to Koh Samui. Ex-backpacker hippy paradise, more recently discovered by the less open-minded but slightly better-off hedonists in search of all-night beach parties and all-day sleeping in the sun at the obvious resort.

But away from the party populist beach there is a peaceful island that has not been spoiled by lager lout reputations. Like any holiday destination, there are charter boats and tourist traps, but it's easy to slip aside from that. A beachfront room on the north coast is as peaceful as the calm sea lapping against soft, palm-lined sand.

This then is home for a while. A chance to recharge and sit with a cool beer, a book and sunglasses, easing my way through the day. A little supermarket across the road will provide most things I need. A fishermen's market a short stroll along the beach will supply fish for a BBQ. Time to chill in the heat.

My bike will be delivered to Darwin on the 21st, although I expect customs clearance will take a little while after that, which is picture-postcard perfect, thanks, as my flight to Australia is booked for the 19th. In the words of Hannibal Smith, "I love it when a plan comes together."

'Easy like Sunday morning' – After two weeks of doing mostly nothing, it's time to rouse my lazy self and prepare for my next move. Days of swimming. Sitting in the sun, reading (three) books and generally doing nothing comes to an end tomorrow. Not before time really. It's been enjoyable to take some time off. Contrary to what you might think, travelling all the time does get difficult at times and mentally as well as physically draining. But I feel rested and ready to go again. It will be good to reacquaint myself with my bike. An overnight flight via Perth will see me deposited in Darwin with a few days to sort out the customs requirements.

Koh Samui has been a relaxing, warm and comfortable venue in which to kick back. I haven't seen a lot of it, which is a bit of a shame, but I've spent very little money, which is good for my antipodean adventure to come. Monday mornings aren't very difficult in my life now, but this one closes the chapter. Packing up my small bag and getting ready to move on brings the familiar sense of anticipation for travelling. There is something fabulous in that thought of not being where I am now, tomorrow. The wanderer in me feels fulfilled when it happens. There's something to be said for stability, but I think it leaves me slightly frustrated with life. Thinking there is so much more to experience, so much more to see. Life isn't forever and time accelerates as I get older, it seems.

I have a few hours to spend waiting for the departure from the island as a warm breeze fills the open boarding lounge. The narrow-bodied turbo prop has more cabin staff than paying passengers. After taxiing under a brooding dark sky, flashes of lightning illuminate the wings as we climb through tumultuous clouds and rough turbulence. This feels like the setting of a low-budget disaster movie. MISSING OVER THE BAY OF THAILAND! Luckily, we arrive safely in Phuket to meet the overnight flight to Australia, without resorting to a Lord of the Flies ending.

Land of the young and free,
Of golden soil and wealth for toil.
Where home is girt by sea and land abounds in nature's gifts, of beauty rich and rare.
Advance Australia fair.

14 AUSTRALIA – DOWN UNDER

Arrival via Perth is a welcome back to an English-speaking culture. Suddenly everything is easy. Darwin welcomes me with hot temperatures and the news that all the plans have gone awry. In a non-Darwinian theory the stars would have aligned and my bike would arrive a day after me. But natural selection is a bit more random than that and now the ship with my bike aboard won't dock in Darwin until approximately the 3rd of November. Damn! Still, there are worse places to be stranded!

A brief look around this little town in the wonderful isolation of the Northern Territory shows there is lots to see and do. On the spur of the moment I hire a small car for a few days to give me the ability to widen my exploration range and get around without having to walk everywhere. It was fine being stuck in one place on a beach, but getting around in Darwin means motorised transport is nice to have. It did, however, provide a scary moment when, after months of driving on the right side of the road, a lapse in concentration meant I ended up on the wrong side of the road, much to the annoyance of the oncoming 'ute' driver. The beaches nearby look utterly wonderful but are equally deadly as it's box jellyfish season. Not a single swimmer in the clear water, under the fabulous blue skies. Anywhere else there would be swimmers, surfers and divers. Swimming is limited to lakes and pools. I suppose that means the shoreline is a place for nature to live undisturbed. It's slightly ironic that, surrounded by acres of pristine beach, Darwin has a wave machine pool in a beachside development.

I do like the 'vibe' in the town. There are lots of backpacker facilities. Outback-equipped trucks and long-haired travelling types rubbing shoulders with the local community. I should fit in easily with my current style statements of third-world cotton shirts and shoulder-length hair! Peace and love, man! So with a couple of weeks to fill I'll take time to explore a little. I've had time enough sat still over the last couple of weeks. I had hoped to be on the east coast in two weeks' time but I'm stuck with it and will still have time to visit the Great Barrier Reef and plenty of other sights in my time here. I've just lost a couple of weeks out of my available time in Australia. 'No worries'.

Discovery Darwin – A few days into my time in Darwin and I'm getting a feel for where I am. Finding your way around a new town is always an interesting time and this small town is no exception. It is a small town. The central district just a couple of miles square, making it easy to navigate and with everything available in town that I might need before I venture into the outback. What I need depends on what the customs man decides I can't bring into the country via the crate containing my bike and travelling gear. I have sourced a replacement rear tyre for the bike at a Kawasaki dealer on the outskirts of town. The tyre has been put to one side for me; I just need the bike to put it on. Checking on marinetraffic.com, which shows the location of ships at sea, at least the ship with my bike on board appears to be en route to Darwin. In the meantime, I've rented another car to get around a bit and have looked up a few tourist destinations to visit while I have the time.

With the weather at a constant sunny 34°C it's summer time, and, despite the empty beaches and waters inhabited by deadly stingers, there are safe places to take a cooling swim. Inland billabongs and cascading waterfalls are apparently a local favourite. I visited a crocodile tourist attraction. The 'swimming with crocs' (in a glass cage) was appealing until I worked out the cost for twenty minutes in the pool. Think I'll save the money, thanks anyway! The 'Darwin waterfront' has a wave pool and a safe harbour for swimming with a small man-made beach and grassy banks. On a hot day during the week it is relatively quiet, and drying off in the sun with my book to read after a cooling dip has been a favourite way to soak up a couple of lazy hours in an afternoon. At this time of year I am more used to the English climate turning towards winter, so it is good to say that the Australian spring is more than pleasant. But then chasing one long summer around the planet has always been part of the plan.

After mooching around Darwin Central for a few days I took a trip out into the 'bush' at an area called Litchfield Park (which sounds more like a horse race track!). It's a 1500km² natural area about 100km south of Darwin. Without the car it would have been mostly inaccessible to me. But after an hour's drive the modern world fell away, to be replaced by low trees with dark lower halves recording the effects of the last bush fire and white new growth branches on top. Apart from an itinerant herd of (cue Aussie accent: bloody big) cattle wandering across the road, causing me to make a dramatic reduction in speed, the countryside seemed a little devoid of wildlife as it baked under a 39°C afternoon. I've yet to see my first kangaroo, but I'm sure my time will come! Passing a sign to 'Lost City' (surely not lost any more, then?) and with nowhere in particular to aim for, the first signpost that didn't specify the need for a 4x4 vehicle pointed me to 'Florence Falls'. In spite of the in-car air-conditioning, the chance to cool off a bit was too good to miss. After a bit of a climb from the viewing platform to get there, it was worth the effort in the heat to enjoy swimming in the plunge pool under a natural power shower. Further on, a second waterfall sign tempted me again to swim at Wangi Falls. When water is in short supply I feel a need to try out every opportunity under the subtropical sun.

Travelling back with the car windows open, I'm trying not to rely on the air-con too much as it doesn't help acclimatisation. I thought about the challenges ahead once my bike arrives. With approximately 2000km to travel to the east coast it will be quite an undertaking, although, having crossed Kazakhstan in July, not one that I'm overly concerned about. And with no need to cover big distances, as I did in Russia, I plan to limit the mileage to manageable levels each day and take my time. There are plenty of fuel stops and roadhouses on the route, so finding a place to stop each evening shouldn't be an issue. Even so, travelling all day in near 40°C temperatures will necessitate a little forward planning for being a bit self-sufficient with water supplies. But that is all to come later. For now, the adventure is exploring this part of the Northern Territory and enjoying the seasonal sunshine.

Doing time in Darwin – The world over, Friday night is the start of the weekend and everybody is out for a beer.

Darwin is no different, apart from the dress code in October is strictly summer attire of shorts and flip-flops, with noisy lorikeets in the tree across the road from Shenannigan's Irish bar selling Guinness and v8 'utes' cruising by. It's not freezing cold downtown Sheffield, but on the flip side it's not party Costa Spain either. Just a few beers in places along the main street, all the pubs with open outdoor seating and beer by the jug. Nice place, no worries! Apart from the slow progress of the ship carrying my bike on the marine traffic tracking website. I'm just restless and ready to move on, nothing I can do about it. I've got to just relax and enjoy the ride.

Sunday morning and sitting in the park reading under a lightly clouded sky with the temperature still in the thirties, just letting the day drift by. An Aussie-rules 'footy' match barks into life, a small local pitch with a single grandstand that I can see from the road. While I'm no football fan, it's an intriguing mix of sports. Football/rugby/American football all rolled into one with what appears to be fairly easy-to-understand rules. It passes twenty minutes of one quarter of the match. Tuesday is Melbourne Cup Day. I'm told the country stops for that particular horse race. Might be worth seeking out a bar with TV to dip into the atmosphere. Not that horse racing lights my fire either! Might even put a little random bet on. You never know your luck! Or maybe you do! A $5 bet on the winning horse pays me $130. Nice!

I've spent a bit of time trying to sort out insurance. It's nigh on impossible to get cover for the bike. There is a compulsory third-party insurance that I will have to obtain somehow from somewhere, but other than that it's the same as Georgia and Kazakhstan; I'm stuck with it. Surprisingly, Australia appears to be a paper trail nightmare of bureaucracy. Not all states recognising the same documentation, and, from replies I've had to emails and phone calls, no one seems to fully understand the system on a countrywide basis. Potentially there is a green card system, but that only appears to be valid for twenty-eight days and only for a specified journey across states. C'mon Australia, sort it out! One country shouldn't have such a confusing system. I've passed through far less civilised countries that manage to be far less complicated.

The ship with my bike is due to dock late on Thursday. I've been told it could take five working days to clear customs and quarantine. Too long but beyond my control. Darwin is draining my resources and I'm getting no benefit from it. It's a good place but I need to move, to travel, to make progress. It's frustrating. I know that sounds frivolous. I'm in a tropical summer in November, stop complaining, but this wasn't the plan. Then again, what was? I'm at the starting gate; I'm just keen to go, and waiting is the hardest part. Guess it's time for another beer!

Hometown Darwin – I've been here that long it's starting to feel like home! Lazy summer days in Darwin. Days of palm trees, sunshine, swimming. Reading in the park. Days of acclimatising, of getting to feel at home. Understanding how Australia works. Familiarity of the town, the bird chirp from the pedestrian crossing, the amusing abbreviated English.

The 'wet' hasn't come yet. It's early November. I heard the locals expect the wet season to be late this year. Bonfire night back home. The 5th of November passes without the usual fireworks and bonfires of my English heritage that celebrate an attempt to blow up Parliament. Surely something amiss there somewhere? However, nature steps in and obliges with a few big rumbles of thunder. Maybe I spoke too soon, but it came to nothing. Unlike the east coast that is being battered by storms. Maybe the delay was meant to be, preventing me from running into the rain.

The ship with my bike on board docked on Thursday. I want to unravel it from the port authorities, have it back in my possession. Customs fees, port charges, quarantine inspections, compulsory insurance, paperwork, paperwork and more paperwork. I'm told after numerous phone calls it will be the middle of next week before I grasp it from the official clutches. I'm being processed. One day after the container ship's arrival and not unexpectedly no update from the port authorities. It's going to be next week. I'm resigned to that. I hope to be on the road before the weekend; it will be good to do so. It seems like a long, long time since I had to travel. The break from travelling in the bay of Thailand was planned. This stationary time in Darwin, though not unpleasant, wasn't. I feel the call of the wild, the escape from civilisation, gazing at uninterrupted stars with nothing to do except ride, experience the distance, feel the isolation and perhaps share an understanding with like-minded travellers.

It's what has made this whole venture worthwhile.

Adventure and experiences outside of normal understanding.

My mind is set to apply that feeling to day-to-day life; it's what makes me feel alive. It makes normality worthwhile and common concerns trivial. We all have a whole world to visit. To explore and to see, and yet so many of us choose to take the safe option. Plan for a future that none of us actually know is actually there. I've said it before, but human life is short with no guarantees. If you live to a healthy old age to spend your pension then that safe option was the right one, but ...

The red light is stale. The amber light is about to illuminate. The starting blocks are calling.

And the beat goes on – It's funny being in a place long enough to peek behind the curtain. Like seeing a stage play. Out front it's bright lights, scenery, actors in character. But take a glance out back and the scenery is propped up on wooded frames and the characters are just costumes.

Darwin on the surface is a buzzing little town. Lots of shops aimed at tourists and backpackers. But the resident population actually appears quite small. The travellers are by nature transient. There's lots of empty shops. Fast food joints competing for the same dollar as their neighbours. This far out, the 'territory' actually appears to be a fairly tough existence, unless you're earning the government dollar. There's a dark subculture of drunken Aboriginals, barefoot and seemingly living on another plane of existence. Angry with society, maybe with good reason. The white colonists have only been here a couple of hundred years, short enough for long memories. Modern white guilt over past conquests won't ease the situation. Things move on; you can't buy forgiveness. Just live with it.

I'm applying pressure to the shipping agent on Monday. Is there anything I need to do to ease my bike out of the port? And so it goes on. I have made some progress on compulsory third-party insurance. Finally someone who seems to know the full SP. Once my bike clears customs and quarantine, I need a compliance check and can apply for temporary CTP insurance. I will need the carnet as well. Damn! That is with the import company in Melbourne. I posted it to them on arrival so they could process the import/export process centrally. Now I need it back! More red tape, more bureaucracy and more actions I need to take. I've got to get an appointment for the compliance check. I can only book that online, estimating when the bike might be released to me and arranging a test slot in the system that is only available at a week's notice. I have to sort out collection once I'm given the go-ahead and get the rear tyre fitted en route from the port to the test, get the carnet delivered to me in Darwin ASAP and then, maybe, I can leave. More time in Darwin yet.

BREAKING NEWS!... BREAKING NEWS!...
BREAKING NEWS!... BREAKING NEWS!...
BREAKING NEWS!... BREAKING NEWS!...
BREAKING NEWS!...

I've visited the import agent that has my bike today,

actually seen the unopened crate. It has cleared customs and is sat in the shipping agent's warehouse waiting for the visit from the quarantine man; it can't be opened before that happens. What's not helping the situation is industrial action by Australia's border control staff, just what I don't need! However, with a bit of luck the inspection will happen very soon. I've also registered with the local Motor Vehicle Registration (MVR) office and booked a compliance inspection slot online, which will allow me to obtain the required compulsory third-Party (CTP) insurance. Not sure how easy that will turn out to be and the next available slot with the MVR is not until Friday. Are you keeping up with this soap opera? I might actually get to see a bit more of Australia than Darwin yet!

Yes worries, mate – Bike unloaded. Quarantine man says may be okay; he's seen worse I only spent two whole days cleaning it up back in Korea until he looks at the front sprocket cover. Grease around the chain and sprocket needs cleaning out. It's a drive chain; it's supposed to be lubricated! He's just doing his job, but it will delay release of the bike and will cost again. Not that I have much choice.

I'm contacted by a local biker, a guy who knows the system. I take a bus ride to his place just outside of town to see if he can expedite the process at all. On board the modern, clean, air-conditioned bus, piped muzak and loud Aboriginal chatter accompany me on my ride. I guess 'Walkabout' means catching the bus in 2015, but it's a wasted journey; he gets no further than I could. The process doesn't progress as the quarantine clean-up takes as long as it takes. No amount of pestering makes any difference. Another phone call to the shipping office tells me it won't be done in time for the scheduled compliance check: another delay in this never-ending debacle. The next available slot at the MVR office is Wednesday. Stonewalled when I call to try to get it in. "You have to book online."

I have now been in Darwin for almost one month. I may have the patience of a saint but I've had enough now. There's a lot more of Australia to see than Darwin but I'm stuck. Pushing to get things done makes no difference, and trying to make things happen just ends in frustration. I have tried to sit back and just let it happen at its own pace, thinking there's no point stressing, but still nothing gets sorted.

Once I get legal in the Northern Territory I will head for Queensland. A journey of a maximum of four days where the hard-won legality in NT becomes void and I have to obtain another set of permits and insurance cover to ride on Queensland's roads. It's a minefield of bureaucracy and conflicting legal systems. I'm just weary of it now and not feeling very positive. I am sure I'll get the feeling back but it's tough to remain in a positive state of mind, so, seeing if I can make any headway with Queensland's Department of Transport to be ahead of the game, I called their customer centre and was referred to their website.

Extract follows:
To drive a vehicle in Queensland that has been imported either using a temporary import approval or a Carnet De

Passage (CDP), you will need an overseas visiting vehicle (OVV) permit.

An OVV permit recognises your overseas registration and allows you to drive the vehicle in Queensland during your visit. There is no fee for an OVV permit.

Your vehicle is only eligible for an overseas visiting vehicle permit while its overseas registration is current. We cannot issue a permit if you aren't able to renew your overseas registration.

How to apply for a permit

To apply for an OVV permit, you need:

- Your current passport
- A Queensland compulsory third party (CTP) certificate
- Your overseas vehicle registration documents
- Your vehicle import approval or your CPD.

Bring all of these documents and your vehicle to a transport and motoring customer service centre. Your vehicle's details will need to be checked and recorded on your permit.

Easy! So next stop, one of the 'list of licensed insurers' –

"No, mate, you need to go to the Department of Transport. We only issue CTP for Australian-registered vehicles." Yeah, been there. They say I need to talk to you. "Sorry, can't help." Do you ever get one of those days? Not moving on!

Wet season cometh – Well, the whole point of getting here when I did was to avoid the wet season, but seeing as I've been here a month and 'the wet' is late, it seems I've ridden my luck too far. A passing thunderstorm this afternoon was a warm-up act to the main event this evening, with biblical rain illuminated by brilliant flashes of lightning backed up by the staccato beat of thunder claps. The tropical heatwave has been brought to a sudden end. No biggie, as they say here, but might make travel and possibly camping an interesting experience once I get moving.

After a weekend of no progress as expected, an early phone call to the warehouse and told of yet more delays. The bike was allegedly cleaned on Friday but failed a further check by another inspector, and, rather than sort it out there and then, it was left over the weekend and will be booked in for another clean and inspection: "maybe today, maybe tomorrow," (deleted swear words). The comedy act continues, with the TV news reports calming Australians after the events in Paris by saying the border controls are 'the best in the world'. I have to say, in my experience, they couldn't organise the proverbial.

In a brief diversion from the trials and tribulations of importing my bike, I order lunch in a cafe. Food delivered to the table, waitress asks, "Do you want any crack with that?" (bemused look from me)... Oh! The pepper mill. English really is a strange language sometimes.

The rainstorms continue on the north-east coast, but Darwin has returned to its hot and sunny state after the weekend storm. I think something in the stars is aligning to make me avoid the worst of the weather in Queensland.

At least I know I'm not the only one going through

this experience as I meet Scottish couple Norman and Elaine in the Motor Vehicle Registration office. They are travelling the world on their Triumph Scramblers and are going through their own similar dramas after importing their bikes by air to Adelaide, before they were transported by road the length of the country to Darwin, where the quarantine inspections were taking place. Future advice for anyone wanting to ride in Australia? Rent or buy a bike when you get here! Not cheap but far easier. But then, where's the challenge in that?

A day of phone calls, non-returned messages, being told the guy I'm dealing with is not in the office; enough is enough. A personal visit proves he is at his desk so I wait in the office for an update. Another phone call to the quarantine office and an hour later I get a call back. I have to be at the shipping agent at 7.30am tomorrow to sort it out. Whatever it takes, my bike is getting sprung from their clutches. With the rest of the legal requirements, a combination of compulsory third-party insurance, Overseas Visiting Vehicles permits, compliance checks and interstate legality to be dealt with after I re-enact *The Great Escape's* leaping-the-wire scene!

Quarantine. The final act – I managed to prise the bike from the vice-like grip of the quarantine man and escaped to freedom! I get to the shipping agents at 7.30am. We drive to the secure holding area for 8am, but the inspector fails to arrive. In the meantime, I strip the bike apart; all the body panels are jet washed with a pressure washer designed to clean container ships rather than a 200kg motorcycle. It is strong enough to take paint off my little travel partner that has already gone through so much as parts are scattered across the yard under the water blast. Back in the office I wait for the inspector, refusing to go anywhere until this gets sorted out. At 10.30am the shipping agent gets a phone call at his desk; there will be an inspector available at midday. Time to go for some breakfast at a nearby café, but only halfway through my cup of coffee a phone call informs me the inspector is there now and to get myself to the bike. At 11.15am I arrive and I'm told he's already been and it has passed! Time to put it all back together and return it on the back of a pick-up to the shipping agent's office. Battery on and it burst into life at the first touch of the starter button. Freedom beckons! Well, partial freedom, the final piece of the jigsaw being the MVR compliance check and the compulsory third-party insurance scheduled for Wednesday. Riding illegally, I call into the motorcycle shop to have the tyre fitted that they reserved for me. The tyre fitter informs me the rear brake pads are knackered, the brake light isn't working, the horn doesn't work, the fork seals are leaking and the rear suspension linkage is seized. Chances of passing the MVR test are none! Back at the hotel I fit a new set of brake pads I have with me. The fork seal is indeed seeping a bit as a consequence of being compressed during the voyage and forcing the fork oil past the rubber seal, but it seems to be okay. I'll live with it for now. A new horn from another shop, an adjustment of the brake light switch and it's good to go, I hope. After all the concerns, the compliance check was little more than a formality. A brief check of the lights and the engine and frame numbers provided a signed certificate and CTP insurance was purchased, giving me the freedom of

Australia's Northern Territory. Don't know what all the fuss was about! Keep on rolling, baby! Finally, after all the delays and bureaucracy.

Moving on – On Thursday I departed Darwin and headed south on the Stuart Highway, passing Litchfield Park again and arriving at Adelaide River. Blazing hot temperatures of 40°C mean the bike is overheating. The water level in the coolant tank is a little low, but the major issue is that the airflow is just not cool enough to keep the engine from getting too hot. Travelling on to Katherine I cover a total of 300km. That's far enough under the searing hot skies to ease me back into the rhythm of travelling after the enforced break. A room with air-con and a cool pool is great, thanks. In extreme contrast to what the European winter will be experiencing under freezing dark winter skies, riding on open stretches of road with super-heated air blowing in your face at nearly 50°C is pretty tough. Taking several rest stops to take on water, I got through four litres during the day. Just like back in Russia the bike continuously overheated slightly, with the water temperature warning light illuminating until I switched off the engine while still rolling, then going out when I restarted. But the air flowing through the radiator was doing little to cool the water flowing around its internals.

Day two on the road – Leaving Katherine at 8am was probably an hour too late. The temperature is already at 30°C. That's comfortable to ride in but that's the coolest part of the day. Not thinking straight, I fuelled up and refilled my water carriers, but completely forgot to investigate the mesh tent I had seen in the window of the town's camping shop until I was on my way. No turning round to go back; I'll find another!

Riding through to Mataranka station, groups of Aboriginal people sit out the heat under the shade of a tree. One asks me the time while waving his iPhone at me. Hang on; I thought you were supposed to know all this stuff by the bark of the old gum tree or the quality of the witchetty grubs or something. Guess that was in the dreamtime before 'bottle shops'.

During a stop for fuel and a cooling rest at a Daly Waters roadhouse, I met Josh riding his KTM 690 Supermoto to Alice Springs. Our paths crossed a couple more times during the day. Everyone takes their rest stops where they can on this route and, despite his speed advantage, Josh is forced to stop more often for fuel and because of the distance limitation of his bike's narrow seat. We continue to play a game of road leapfrog throughout the rest of the day.

After reaching the beat-up and run-down township of Elliot on the Stuart Highway I decide it seems prudent to move on. With its fuel station burnt out, Elliot is not a place you'd choose to stop. I ride on through Renner Springs and Banka Banka to the Threeways Roadhouse at the junction with the Barkly Highway. A mix of truck stop, camp ground, motel and a place to rest once the sun goes down. A basic hut accommodation is the last one they have available. Thanks.

An early start at 6.30am under cloudless skies at about 24°C is pleasant! 180 easy km later and a breakfast stop at Barkly Homestead Roadhouse is probably the nicest place I've seen on this part of the journey. The temperature goes over 30°C at 9am. Horrible hot side winds blight the journey across a flatland of stunted vegetation. Two dust twisters follow me for a while, a black dust cloud being dragged into the sky on a tube of rotating hot air. The tarmac blisters in the sun as the temperature rises to a steady 48°C after a lunch stop at Camooweal Roadhouse just over the Queensland border, where a sign proclaims 'Welcome to Queensland. Set your watch five years and thirty minutes ahead' – it wasn't exactly the height of twenty-first century technology in Camooweal either!

One thing most people won't experience in the pollen-filtered, air-conditioned atmosphere of a car is the pungent waft of the numerous large animal road kills that litter the Barkly Highway as they slowly desiccate on the hot tarmac. Buzzards and harriers seem to prefer their meat well done. About two days in the sun tenderised by a few road trains, thanks. I've seen lots of 'roos now, just no live ones. Is there any 'wet' at all involved in the wet season, I wonder? After the last two days I would hate to see the dry!

On Sunday I slept late after arriving in the first big town over the border. Mount Isa is a lead, zinc, silver and copper mining town that grew from the settlers displacing the region's Aboriginal tribes in 1884. A little motel on the edge of town was an oasis of cool after a very hot day's riding. By the time I woke it was too late to move and I make a decision to take Sunday as a rest day. I know that seems a bit lightweight, but two fairly tough days after six weeks off the bike drained my energies and fried my senses and dehydration dulled my sensibility. No point taking unnecessary risks or pushing too hard to make up lost time. There's still enough days in the month. The east coast is almost within reach, but I also need to speak to the local Transport and Motoring Service Centre about the Overseas Visiting Vehicle (Aus acronym time – OVV) and they aren't open until Monday, so it feels like the right thing to do. On Monday morning I'll call in, obtain the permit and move on. After a chat with a couple of blokes in the bar (it's hard not to fall into a really bad Aussie accent with some of these phrases!) it seems my original route via Normanton is probably not the best idea. It sounds similar to Elliot and is certainly a place to pass right on by. So I think I'll now travel on towards Townsville to get me to the coast quicker, then make my way towards Port Douglas for a couple of days.

I'm at the roads office when they open at 8am; it is the usual palaver of paperwork and red tape. The woman behind the desk appears to have had her sense of humour burnt out by the hot sun. She demands proof of my Queensland address. The only thing I can offer is a receipt from the motel. That does the job and I'm legal to travel in Queensland. After, she has a quick look at my compulsory third-party insurance certificate. It doesn't actually state that it is only valid in the Northern Territory and, as the nice lady in the Queensland roads office failed to mention it, I decide to play it dumb from here on in and make an 'assumption' that I am legal anywhere in Australia. It's too much effort to go through this in every state. If I get stopped by a policeman I will play the innocent foreigner. As it never happens during the rest of my time in Australia it's not a problem. Did I travel illegally? – yes, probably. Should you? – I can't advise anyone on that subject; that was just my decision at the time. Right or wrong, it was not the first time on the whole journey I accepted that my legality was a little suspect.

After the delays with the roads office I leave Mount Isa too late in the day to make any meaningful distance. A lady in the supermarket suggests my ride is one I should have saved for the winter. That's not something I've ever heard before, back in the icy wasteland of a Yorkshire winter! I get as far as Hughenden late in the day. The Grand Motel is boarded up, but a basic motel on the edge of town provides an overnight bed and rest enough for a 6.30am start the next day.

After pushing on through the heat of the Barkly Highway, the temperature got more temperate the closer I got to the coast, until just north of Townsville the world turned green again, the road winding its way through banana and sugar cane plantations. Rivers with actual water and the pleasantly warm breeze carrying the scents of flora in full summer bloom.

With a ride of over 800km in one day, Cairns is my stop for a couple of days. After chasing an available room in a town full of teenage backpackers and full hostels, I find a room in a backstreet motel and sleep long and well.

The next day I wander around this seaside town, as groups of youngsters gather around the public pool near the seafront, the beach obviously off limits at this time of year.

There are cauldrons of flying foxes in the fig trees, roosting during the day in the trees around Cairns centre, where summer is constant. Winter temperatures are around 26°C and summer at 34°C; I've found the perfect location for anyone suffering from the winter blues. Move to North Queensland; it's a place where summer and winter are relative terms and sunshine is readily available year round. After my first proper rest day since I set off from Darwin that isn't heat-induced, I treat myself to a Barramundi fish supper with a $10 AUD beer to wash it down.

The pelican brief – There are some. (I can't be much briefer!)

The one-hour ride north from Cairns is along a lovely coastal road, with sweeping corners that reward me with stunning views of palm-lined beaches and clear waters. Up to the picturesque town of Port Douglas, where the town's development hasn't impacted the natural beachfront. Sea, sand and palm trees show that a town doesn't need to build concrete sea promenades and lose what nature created to provide a wonderful connection with the ocean. A fabulous apartment right on the town's main street has a quiet courtyard behind it with a shaded pool and an underground car park for my bike. I might never leave!

A day trip out to Kuranda National Park starts with an amazing cable car ride over the incredible scenery of the North Queensland rainforest. There are stunning views as the car travels at tree canopy height through the trees, passing waterfalls and rivers, with stop-off points along the way to take in the sights and sounds of the wonderful, breathtaking scenery. The whole journey is eye-poppingly, spectacularly stunning! Kuranda village survives as a tourist attraction, the village in the rainforest, a bohemian alternative to modern life; but its history comes from timber, a resource that is heavily protected these days. I made the return journey by rail, a steam locomotive rumbling along a scenic line across gorges and through tunnels, originally built to transport timber workers into the hills. A journey that took twice as long as the cable car to travel back to my start point. While I thought that excursion would be difficult to top, and while I was in the mood for some tourist-style trips, I also booked a day out on the Great Barrier Reef. A swift boat whisked the paying passengers out to three reef destinations, where groups of first-time and experienced scuba divers set off for the deeper parts of the reef, leaving us lesser mortals to explore with relative freedom wherever our swimming ability took us. Wrapped in a stinger-protective full-body Lycra suit, and equipping myself with an underwater camera, I managed to capture at least a slight impression of what was on view in this amazing underwater ecosystem.

East Coast Capricorn one – After the tourist time in tropical North Queensland it was time to start my journey south. Reluctantly leaving Port Douglas at 9.30am, I travelled back towards Cairns and on to Townsville, which I bypassed on my way north. An overnight stop, camping for free in the Bushy Parker rest area, gave me the opportunity to get a bit closer to the sounds of night-time Australia during a hot night, using a new tent I acquired in Cairns which has a mesh side. Having failed to purchase one back in Katherine, it was a must-buy if I hoped to stay cool overnight. It also offered a wonderful view of the night sky and a vast natural umbrella of vivid stars to sleep beneath.

I saw eternity the other night.
Like a great ring of pure and endless light,
All calm as it was bright,
And round beneath it time in hours, days, years,
Driven by the spheres, Like a vast shadow moved in
the world And all her train were hurled.

Henry Vaughan, The World

Having passed through Ayr travelling along the Bruce
Highway through to Mackay in this little reminiscence
of Scotland, the road passes through a flatter section
just inland from the Whitsunday Islands at the southern
tip of the Great Barrier Reef. An overnight stop at the
foreboding-sounding campsite at Midge Point was
thankfully free of biting insects, but did provide my first
sighting of a wallaby and a kookaburra before reaching
Rockhampton, where it's time for a little more motorcycle
maintenance. A Kawasaki dealer in town sorts out the oil
and filter change it has desperately needed for a while.
Changing the oil and filter myself, around the back of a
hotel in Russia, was relatively easy. Disposing of used oil
in the back car park of a motel in Australia might be a bit
more difficult.

Not much to tell about Rockhampton. It is apparently
the beef capital of Queensland. More interesting to me was
that it sits on the Tropic of Capricorn. From here south
the climate eases a little. Surprisingly, it doesn't take long
to feel the effects as the temperature 'plummets' to around
20°C. By the time I reach the un-sunny sunshine coast
I've worn my textile bike trousers for the first time since

Russia. A caravan campsite by the beach at Maroochydore is okay. The town is named after the Aboriginal name for the area as the home of the red-billed swans that inhabit the coast. It's not a particularly peaceful place to stop, but as an overnight rest it's acceptable enough and close to Australia Zoo.

Australia Zoo is different to most zoos I've visited. Getting up close and personal with the animals is the zoo's formula, in just the same way that the founder Steve Irwin used to: crikey! Big crocs, 'roos and koalas are the big draw for the audiences, but all of Australia's fauna is on display and accessible to all, in addition to African giraffes and zebras, which have massive enclosures to roam, and a Sumatran tiger enclosure built to resemble the Cambodian Angkor Wat temple complex.

Civilisation, Jurassic coasts and GP heroes – The next stop was Brisbane, where I met up with Simon, the friend who had been one of the trip's points I had planned from the very start of this adventure. After picking up his rented BMW F700 bike we will ride to his adopted home town of Melbourne. Brisbane is a relatively small city and leaving it was fairly easy, and a steady day's travel brought us to Byron Bay, a lovely little seaside town with a hippy vibe, surf on the beach and flying foxes over the campsite. There are definitely a few folks wandering barefoot around town that 'dropped in and dropped out', man! I wanted to stay longer than the two nights to enjoy the atmosphere a bit, but due to Simon's limited time there is a need to cover the miles. Not what I had in mind, but, apart from dropping out of the timetable that Simon has, there's not much I can do.

The bike had been feeling a little odd and a bit of

investigation showed up a knackered rear wheel bearing. Luckily, I have a spare set of bearings and it was easily repaired with the aid of a socket extension and a makeshift brick hammer, although I found it a little strange that the efficient fitter back in Darwin had failed to notice that little issue on his list of broken items.

An overnight stop at Urunga was a cool place to stop, and with perfect timing the heavens opened not long after pitching the tent. After tea in the local pub a walk along the coastal boardwalk was a perfect lookout point to spot wild kangaroos and marvel at the multi-directional waves as they broached the sandbar that had brought about the demise of several sailing ships when the area was heavily used as a trading port.

The next day's journey was through some wonderful coastal roads, forested lands meeting crystal azure waters of coastal inlets with wooded shores providing a cool ride through the heat of the day. With a vague plan to camp lakeside towards the end of the day, the weather played a part in the decision as a tropical storm moved in, forcing an overnight stop at a little hotel in small-town Australia. I almost expected the sheriff to ride into town to stir up a posse to ride down the cattle rustlers. It was all a bit wild west!

Riding down through the town of Newcastle, complete with its own (prettier version) of Wallsend, and down the coast towards the beautiful Australian Lake District, where cool air temperatures and shaded roads snake alongside crystal clear lakes, it is a fabulous part of the world to ride through. Staying off the main highway as much as possible added to the distance between towns and destinations, but the scenery and sudden explosion of amazing views as you travel along are more than worth it, each sublime view surpassing the last in a never-ending competition for the most astounding vista. A stretch of dusty dirt road through sub-tropical forest eventually ended up back on the main tarmac road heading into Sydney. The inevitable build-up of urban traffic feels magnified after the glorious space of the country roads, but the Harbour Bridge and Opera House are a required photo opportunity even if the shouty security man was less than happy with me riding right up through a pedestrian area to get them! Never mind – I'm moving on – thanks!

South of Sydney we forgo the opportunity to pass Bondi Beach, but having seen Surfers Paradise I don't feel like I missed much. Another coastal road diversion takes us towards Wollongong, the industrial home town of former Grand Prix world motorcycle champion Wayne Gardner, the highlight being the road into town along a coastal bridge, before finding a peaceful campsite at Killalea State Park. The swarms of flies in the morning driving me to distraction as I packed the tent away was like some game show trial! Of more concern was another bike issue, and, despite adjusting and lubricating the chain before leaving, the safety of the ride was badly compromised by the state of the drive chain. I decided that I had pushed it as far as I dare on this journey. A really bad tight spot meant that if I adjusted it correctly at that point it was almost loose enough to be able to jump off the sprockets at its slackest point. Stopping at a motorcycle shop at Nowra was well worth it as a new chain and drive sprockets were purchased and fitted for about the same price as buying them in the UK. The bike massively improved afterwards and my fear of being launched down the road with a locked rear wheel was cast aside. To get all the way to the east coast of Australia on one chain, through the desert, heat, rain, gravel and dust I have gone through on the way is amazing. The automatic lubrication system undoubtedly helped initially, but that gave up months ago and my attempts at maintenance obviously paid dividends in the end.

With yet more amazing countryside to travel through, the crystal clear azure waters at the town of Lakes Entrance burst into view as the road twisted and turned through the wooded hillsides. A town named Eden promised a lot but delivered little and, just the other side, the wide open space of a beachside campsite provided a place to pitch up and have a camp fire. Rushing onwards the next day, heading further south, brought us onto Wilsons Promontory, known as The Prom and named after a London merchant in 1798. A drive along the peninsula led to a campsite at Tidal River, a place that could easily be from the Jurassic period with a long sweeping beach and not surprisingly a tidal river! The local wildlife, obviously used to human occupation, was not put off by tents and camping activity, with wallabies and wombats getting close enough to undermine the tent overnight.

The next day was an easy ride to Phillip Island, the venue of the Australian MotoGP and world superbike rounds and a place I've wanted to get to for a while. It was an interesting visit despite it not being a race weekend, the motor museum and gift shop providing enough entertainment for this slightly overawed visitor to the furthest distant race track I will ever visit. Sadly, a race school event meant getting into the circuit was not possible, but the visitor centre and a view of the circuit was enough. Sadly, camping overnight at nearby Cowes was not as peaceful as the surrounding coastal landscapes. After the rush to get from Brisbane to Melbourne, due to the limited time that Simon had available, I was keen to get back to my own less time-constrained schedule. So, after a couple of days of staying at Simon's place that included his work's Christmas 'do', it was good to get back on the road and make my own decisions.

The Great Ocean Road – From the bay ferry at Queenscliffe the temperature rose to the high 30s°C as I travelled west for about the first time since I left home. Torquay and Anglesey passed without sight of any camping facilities, although those two places are at least closer together than they are in the UK as the Great Ocean Road twisted and turned around the coastline, rainforest on my right and rolling surf on my left. At a point where riding in the heat became uncomfortable, a few clouds rolled in and cooler weather made progress a little easier; and, as the skies darkened, a campsite in Lorne provided what I needed just when I needed it. I'm still not sure how that happens, but it has been a regular feature of the whole journey. Maybe there is something to be said for cosmic ordering, and my thoughts went back to a conversation with Marco on board the ship across the Caspian Sea.

Lorne is a little seaside town with a couple of pleasant rivers meandering down to a long, shallow beach with rolling waves and some sense of being there for a while. One thing Australia lacks is any olde worlde charm. With the majority of buildings only a few years old, you won't find cobbled streets leading to an historic harbour, but the rainforested coastline and easy pace of life are a pleasure to be enveloped in.

I've had to make a few decisions about how the rest of the trip will unfold and after a few investigations about shipping the bike to New Zealand, the cost simply isn't worth doing. So I've decided to use some of the money saved to hire a camper van in NZ and fly myself home by continuing east, to complete the circumnavigation of the planet. Time and money are both at a premium and riding across the USA isn't feasible with what I've got. I'm not spent up, but it's not a bottomless pit and I don't want to arrive back in the UK on Friday and go back to work on Monday, but that's for the future. For now I have the Great Ocean Road to ride towards Adelaide and that's just fine, thanks.

Sunday is cool, less than 20°C, and a pleasant summer's day is broken after lunch by persistent rain. The local cinema, est. 1937 and never modernised, it seems, is showing *Star Wars Episode VII*; well, there's nothing spoiling, so why not? But it's just a clichéd rehash of the original story and the sun is out by the time it's over. Time to move on tomorrow; Lorne has been a pleasant reintroduction to life on my own, but travel is the overriding necessity, sitting still just a pause between stages of the journey.

The road twists and turns from the coast through rainforest with huge prehistoric-style ferns and massive, twisted trees. It is a sight to behold and one I try to fix in my mind, but like many others it will be washed from memory as time passes. The Twelve Apostles is an impressive coastline of eroding limestone stacks, except there aren't twelve any more as nature takes its course, with only eight left standing. The advertising brands it as 'The world's most dramatic coastline': quite a statement! Half of the population of South East Asia seem to be drawn to the viewing hotspots, which necessitates a jostling of position to get a photo in between the selfie sticks and pouting poses for smartphone and iPad shots. Luckily, I possess my own way of rising above the masses! A small hillside campsite overlooking the Gellibrand River provides a restful night not far from the remaining pillars of limestone, where the sound of the ocean carries round the headland and up the river valley to lull me to sleep. The ride through picturesque Port Campbell and along the rest of the Ocean Road is uneventful apart from a brief stop at Port Fairy, where a gentleman from Malaysia thrusts $10 into my hand and tells me to buy myself a good meal after taking photographs of my bike with his wife/daughter. Not sure if he thinks I'm either poor or undernourished or both! The road eventually leads me past Portland and on to Cape Bridgewater which will be my destination for the Christmas weekend. A stroll along the beach on Christmas Day will be a pleasure, although it will be a challenge in the chilled Southern Ocean to manage my ritual of swimming in every sea I have travelled along so far. Australia's south coast is reminiscent of the UK's north-east coast, it seems, with 'bracing' winds and cold sea, the Southern Ocean keeping temperatures down along the coast.

Cape Christmas – Christmas Eve had seen me walk

around the headland taking in the sights of the coast, with a fur seal colony and what is known locally as the 'petrified forest' but is, in fact, a collection of limestone tubes created from water collection and erosion. Similarly, Christmas Day came and went with little sign of festivity. Surfers surfed and campers camped with little sign of huge turkey dinners, bloated Christmas puddings or excessive beer consumption. A lovely cooked breakfast was accompanied by Christmas tunes and cracker hats, but otherwise my day was unremarkable, filled with a walk along the Cape Bridgewater beach filling my lungs with fresh salty air, feeling the breeze of a balmy summer's day. All a very sharp contrast to the commercial and hugely interpreted importance of a single day at the end of December in the depths of the European winter. Maybe the lights, the huge amounts of food and alcohol, the gathering of friends and family are symbols of a deep need to fend off the harsh winter's darkness and conversely it doesn't have the same driving force in the warmth of a southern-hemisphere summer. Whatever the actual truth, the relevance is somehow lost to me as I watch the surf rolling onto the long beach with a cold beer to hand and a lack of appetite after the hearty cooked breakfast. Imagine celebrating Christmas with all its attendant trappings while you are on your summer holiday at the seaside and maybe you can get some understanding of my point of view.

News arrives late on Christmas Day that the glorious ancient flora of the Otway Park that I had travelled through along the Great Ocean Road a few days ago was burning fiercely, as an uncontrolled bush fire raged towards Lorne. It will be sad to see what the effect has been when I retrace my steps in the New Year. A cool and blustery Boxing Day dawns and a traditional walk, albeit in a non-traditional place, breathes new life into the non-festive season. From Bridgewater Lake, a sandy path reaches out to towering sand dunes and a fierce windswept beach littered with the flotsam and jetsam of a little visited landing of crashing waves. Standing on the peak of a dune taking in the fury of nature's unconstrained strength on what is a relatively calm day, it's easy to imagine the huge undertaking it must have been for the European settlers to land on these shores only a couple of hundred years ago, the numerous known shipwreck sites illustrating how fragile human life is against the whim of wind and wave.

Life has been easy over the last few days. My Christmas treat, with a comfortable bed, a sunlit sitting room and wonderful cooked breakfasts served by the friendly host of the Seaview Lodge. The random meeting of fellow guests at a concurrence of journeys. Sometimes chatting, sharing their experiences, sometimes self-engrossed, mobile phone in hand. Aussies, Germans, Japanese, Brits, most on holiday escapes from winter climates. Moving on will happen and moving up the coast, the landscape becomes a little more remote. I'm planning to head as far west as Kangaroo Island just short of Adelaide, before I turn around and get back to Melbourne. Not sure where I will see the New Year arrive yet; as usual, something will turn up.

Twenty Sixteen – human memories are such fragile things, day-to-day senses lost in the fog of time. Photographic snapshots that didn't get processed to paper, cast adrift to infinity and vaguely remembered with no clarity; life is only now. Past experience of little consequence unless it's a lesson learned. Future expectation out of sight. There is no window on what you've seen, no way to review or replay that moment. But it's there, a part of what makes you, the moment gone but the impression stamped on our existence.

Mark Dalton – December 2015

Go west (Not the '80s pop band) – Moving west up the south coast, following in the footsteps of Henry Cole's *World's Greatest Motorcycle Rides* television series, I recognise some of the town's names that I saw on the Australian episode. An overnight stop near the coast turns into trial by ants and I move on, the problem being that every kilometre west I travel is now another kilometre to travel back east to Melbourne. With the desire to push on somewhat diminished, I land at Meningie on the shores of Lake Albert. After 200km of heat, dried-up rivers and salt water marshes, through places with names like Saltwater Creek and along a seemingly endless road, it is a little oasis of cool water, rushes, pelicans and shady trees to pitch the tent under. That's far enough.

Buggles (as in video killed…) – A disaster has befallen my ability to edit the video I've been shooting all along. For a while, the editing software I've been using has failed to recognise the different video formats I'm shooting on different cameras, for no obvious reasons that I could find. After spending far too long figuring it out, it suddenly started working again, except the PC now inexplicably has no sound. A Windows 10 upgrade occurred while I had Wi-Fi connection in Cape Bridgewater and a bit of Google time suggested it may be an incompatibility with that. A not happy couple of hours reverting to the previous version failed to resolve it. I think the sound card may have overheated as the laptop is very hot at that point. For the less PC-literate amongst us, the simple fact is I can't edit the videos I have at present. So for now they have come to a grinding halt. Having published videos to YouTube all the way along this journey, it's a little disappointing.

Earth, wind and fire (not the '70s disco band!) – New Year arrives with 40°C heat and a warm wind that fails to cool over the shallow lake waters. There is an absolute fire ban in place and no one is allowed to create a spark in the tinder-dry South Australian land. With the earth dry from an ongoing drought, the lakes not connected to the sea are reduced to drying salt plains under the heat of the summer sun. Some Aussies, though, find ways of keeping cool while they compete with the pelicans for their fish supper by fishing from deckchairs submerged in the water.

'The Sunset' (The Moody Blues) – As the sun sets on 2015 its time to look back a little at the journey that has been an adventure of a lifetime, with more still to come as 2016 opens its doors. New Zealand early in the New Year and on to the USA for a brief stop along the way. Sadly, those two parts of the trip will occur without my trusty motorbike, which will begin its journey back to Blighty soon, assuming the old country has not been blown away or submerged in winter storms or, indeed, overrun by the European immigrant crisis filling the news headlines.

Don't look back (Boston) – From a rainy start in France around our planet to South Australia, where the year plays out its final card. What an incredibly amazing journey it has been to here. My bike has withstood everything I've thrown at it, including a tram track in Irkutsk. It has suffered my neglect and managed to keep going through 40+°C heat. I've used three rear tyres, two fronts. One set of brake pads, front and rear. One chain and sprocket set. Two oil and filter changes and one set of rear wheel bearings. It has now covered somewhere in the region of 50,000km or 31,000 miles, so I've doubled its lifetime mileage in eight months on the road. I've broken more electrical gadgets and cables than I can remember. My tent has seen years of use in this single trip and I've had more time to think about myself than could sometimes be considered healthy. I've discovered what makes me tick and what ticks me off. I've met adventurers who share the same thoughts of just doing it and others who don't and never will understand.

Don't stop thinking about tomorrow (Fleetwood Mac) – This is a life-affirming adventure that just takes the courage to let your normal life go for a while and forgo your daily rituals and soap operas. At least once in your life take the time to have a real adventure, however small that might be. Take a risk, jump in with both feet and see where it takes you. Travel as much as you can, as far as you can, as long as you can. Life isn't meant to be lived in one place and in the end everything will be fine. If it's not fine now, it's not the end!

My talk with Marco back on the Caspian Sea crossing brought the idea of cosmic ordering into my mind. Something I hadn't considered, but had experienced during my journey. It's not something I am conscious of, but there does seem to be a power at work sometimes when you need it most. You could call it luck or coincidence, but it makes me wonder. What are the chances that something happens when you need it to on your journey through life? Is there a path that each life follows? I don't think I will ever know. All that matters is that if there is a beam that guides my life it knows the way and I don't have to know it exists because it knows me.

Retracing steps – All these little preambles have at one point or another bubbled to the surface as I contemplate my way along the road, marvelling at nature's magnificence or man's ineptitude. Some of these words actually made sense to me at the time. If they don't to you, dear reader, simply pass on by. They are, after all, mostly the ramblings of an overactive, stress-free mind!

January (high summer – how odd) – Saturday after the New Year dawned cool with overcast skies and temperatures at around 16 °C. After the recent numbers, that felt bloody cold to me! With the wind making up for the lack of effort from the temperature, the ride heading back east along the same bumpy, dull road I passed along my way westward was challenging. Gusty winds mixed with salt swept from the dried lakes picked me up as I leant into corners and then just as suddenly dropped, making smooth progress difficult.

More hill than mountain – Along the road to Mount Gambier I decided to look for some camping availability, and while I was parked roadside checking my maps I was asked if I was looking for the race circuit. No, I wasn't, but is there one and what's the occasion? It turns out there is a classic race meeting at Mac Park, a little circuit just outside town; decision made and a campsite secured. Sunday's races look interesting, with classes for older 1960s bikes and younger classics like the 1990s superbikes. It should be good, or would have been as I got to the circuit on Sunday morning to be told the races had been cancelled because sadly a rider had died in a pre-event race the previous afternoon.

So with a spare day it was time to explore the interesting volcanic area around Mount Gambier. Where an amazing blue lake fills the remains of a volcanic crater and the overheard quote of the day was from an American teenager who stood looking at an information board overlooking said volcanic crater and asked, "Okay, where's the volcano?"… Kids!

I'm still heading east and I feel in no rush to get back to Melbourne. Stopping at Port Fairy, where no one was dressed in pink, a week-long music festival was in full swing, with a folk band playing on the grassy main street corner in the centre of town and the local bars advertising evening musical entertainment. There are a lot of local Irish references and many republican flags in evidence. I guess most of Australia's different regional cultural differences go back to the homelands of the original European settlers. During a walk along the wildly windy beach I came across a recently dead bird washed up in the rough surf that I didn't recognise. A later internet reference showed that it was a relatively rare giant petrel. Sometimes these little finds feel like my own discovery; I can't begin to imagine what the original explorers must have felt documenting new species of plants and animals. Back on the campsite at the sports ground just outside of the town, a bloke camping with his family in their 'ute' and a massive tent set-up wanders over to chat about my English-registered bike. After explaining the journey, he thought my trip was "RIPPER", "CRIKEY, MATE!"

Riding back along the Twelve Apostles coastline gave me the opportunity to get some pictures of places I'd ridden past on the way west. Despite my belief that the childhood nursery rhyme was a lie, it seems London Bridge has indeed fallen down. One limestone pillar had been named because it was connected to its neighbour by a natural stone bridge. It was a tourist attraction with a path from the cliff, and reading about it later there was actually a tourist trapped on the rock by the collapse who had to be rescued by helicopter.

Back at the Gellibrand River at Princetown, where I stopped on my way east, I explored the valley a little more and found a cheap, peaceful campsite nearer the coast. In the evenings a mob of kangaroos wandered through at dusk, with two bigger males watching over the rest of the group as they grazed unafraid of the nearby humans, right up to my tent.

After a couple of days relaxing in the peace of the valley I rode through the amazing Otway Park region, marvelling again at the flora and fauna of the area, with koalas and kookaburras in the trees, before arriving in

Apollo Bay, which sounds like it ought to be the location of an Australian soap, where I will prepare for the final run to Melbourne and my exit to New Zealand. Camping next to a small tidal inlet at the 'rec' ground on the edge of town, I applied a whole tin of boot polish to my bike boots, so hopefully they have some water resistance once I wear them again back in the UK. My last night of camping on this trip is something that feels a bit sad. Packing up gear, deciding what I need to keep, what I need to carry with me on the rest of my journey and what I can jettison. When it became too much to think about, a stroll into town and a fish and chip supper on the seafront followed by a bottle of beer back at the tent settled my mind for a good night's sleep after a lovely sunny evening.

The morning dawned and with it the heavy heart of a feeling of the end of a big part of this journey. I packed up the tent for the last time. It has taken a lot of abuse on the trip but survived almost intact: just a few small holes here and there and the stitching on the zip has partially given way. I left it at a charity shop on the way out of town; maybe someone else will find use for it. The sunshade that had served me so well in an endless variety of configurations was left by the bin in the campsite. I like to think maybe someone rescued it for further use. A tin of chain lube, the prop stand I had used to lift the bike off the ground were abandoned to minimise the packing-up. How can I be emotionally attached to small everyday items! After pulling myself together I rode through the burnt out areas of River Wye, affected by the Christmas bush fire. The holiday crowds, oblivious to the fire blackened remains around the campsites, just getting on with their family holidays.

A B&B in Geelong on the road to Melbourne on the west coast of the bay provides the final overnight stop before I get to the shipping agent's at Tullamarine, where I hand over my faithful travel partner to their care for its journey home without me; see you safely back in London, I hope. A taxi ride to the airport is punctuated by a conversation with the Asian taxi driver who doesn't understand why I would do this journey. Yeah, I won't even try to explain; never mind! I have a long wait at the airport until the flight departure at 11.55pm, which gives me time to contemplate what brought me this far. So as the sun sets on my antipodean adventure, the land of the long white cloud beckons, where I will be less an adventurer and more just another hired camper van.

15 NEW ZEALAND – AOTEAROA

With a night that only lasted three hours on the red-eye flight from Melbourne, I lost two more hours as I took another step towards the International Date Line. It was a tough start to my New Zealand adventure; arriving in the early morning hours at Auckland seemed more like a continuation of the same day as Monday melted into Tuesday with a lack of any meaningful sleep. I managed to clear customs without getting arrested for fruit smuggling, or any other potentially hideous food or natural substance! 5.30am local time is 3.30am Australian time, and I can tell! A grey, overcast sky and a desire to getoutta town meant I drove further than I intended after inadvertently getting onto a remote coastal road. A snatched twenty-minute doze at the beautifully peaceful Kawakawa Bay allowed me to drive on. But there are signs all over any free camping places saying no non self-contained campers, which are vans without their own waste disposal systems. According to a local guy I spoke to the day after, it's down to lots of issues with mess from backpacking students in rent-a-campers, just like mine! I wasn't initially overly impressed with the vehicle as rather than a proper camper van it is a converted Toyota Estima. Sold as a Toyota Previa back in Europe, it is a family people carrier, with the back seats removed and replaced by a bed frame and supplied with cooking and camping equipment. It's not so bad and definitely easier than a tent. It's just a shame that what seems to be a turbine smooth electric motor under the bonnet doesn't sound or feel like the 3.0 litre V6 behemoth that it is, and, although the supplied equipment seems new, my first stop for shopping at the town of Thames provided a few cleaning solutions, and some patchouli oil freshened up the interior of my carvancamper transport. Driving on, I arrived at Paeroa, where a horse race track was my overnight stop for $5 NZD. Although I'm pretty sure I would have slept through a full-on race meeting, it provided a peaceful location for the night as I caught up on my missed sleep.

Wednesday dawned cool, and with it a flat battery on the carvancamper. Guess I need to be careful about leaving interior lights on or charging cameras and phones. A jump start from a fellow camper got the motor running as I headed out on the highway, where the sun shone on some dramatic scenery as the day got better. As did my ability to see the world without the fug of sleep deprivation, making life seem somewhat easier and improving my perception of what at first was a slightly sad feeling, mostly due to lack of sleep, but also from leaving my trusty motorbike behind. I'm suddenly inconspicuous, no UK-plated motorbike parked next to a tent, no one notices as I pull up at the petrol station. What used to be a big talking point at every stop is gone. It almost makes me want to shout out that I'm not just another tourist; it's been a big adventure to get here. I don't know, maybe that is what I am now!

Waterfalls, rushing rivers and jagged hilltops with winding roads; New Zealand, it seems, is Australia with interesting scenery! Something like Wales and Scotland and Norway all mixed up together. Slartibartfast might have won an award for this place too, but I'm not hitchhiking. The Bay of Plenty, just as the name suggests, provides everything I need, from a dramatic mountain backdrop to fabulous seascapes, a supermarket with cheap New Zealand Merlot and a soothing river alongside a grassy campsite. I might never move on!

Summer on the North Island is comparable with a European summer so far. One day grey and overcast, the next sunny and warm. As the weather is influenced by the sea there are a lot of similarities. Further south, just like further north at home, is cooler and wilder by all accounts. We shall see. Travelling through the fabulous hills and lakes of New Zealand's North Island is amazing, but I'm disconnected from the elements in a car, which is an inefficacy to me. That connection with the sun, the air and the land (and the rain) is what makes travelling by bike so thrilling. So utterly involving. The roads through this part of New Zealand are made to be travelled by bike, with twists and turns uphill and through valleys. It's my one big disappointment, but, having made the (correct) decision, I've just got to live with it. I'm just feeling the difference of being just another camper on the trail.

New Zealand's thermal activity is not something I had anticipated. The geology, I guess, is obviously volcanic if you look at it... I hadn't, but it is very active, which I suppose is better than dormant if you live on top of a ticking eruption. The town of Rotorua has more than its fair share of thermal pools, bubbling mud and sulphurous steam all wrapped up in a pleasant park experience; just don't wander off the path. No need for KEEP OFF THE GRASS signs here.

Overnight rain lulled me to sleep until the gentle tap of raindrops turned into the crescendo of a torrential downpour that thumped me awake in the early hours. Leaving under a leaden sky after breakfast, I drove through eye-popping, epic scenery of hills and lakes, huge trees and open skies to the rapid-flowing waters at Huka Falls. The blue-white water forced through a narrow channel as if to illustrate that nature will force its own will on the land we stand on. Jet boats ferry tourists to the foot of the cascade to give an experience of the natural power at work.

Driving through the scenic lakeside town of Taupo, it was too early to stop for the night. With huge campers taking up all the best shoreside spots, my little carvancamper shrunk in their company and we moved on, finally parking up for an overnight stop in the scenic little town of Turangi, which appears to have a large Maori population. The old lady running the slightly rundown campsite wanted to talk about everything and explained the ancient un-roadworthy campervan in the corner of the plot was for sale after the old fella who lived there for years had died. The classic truck it was based on would sell to a collector somewhere for lots of money. My amusing moment of the night was the campsite unisex shower block, which had cubicles equipped with glass doors. So much for privacy!

The road to Palmerston climbed high on to the rooftop of the world as I passed Mount Ngauruhoe, which was used as the setting for Mount Doom! I hadn't considered that New Zealand was used extensively for locations for the *Lord of the Rings* films; as such, there are lots of places that have since become tourist attractions, and, seeing as I now fit that appellation, there are definitely a couple of those I would like to include. So, with a ferry crossing booked for Friday, I ended up with a free day, and after a little investigation I found that the location of the film set for Rivendell, which is the home of the elven folk in the stories, was relatively nearby. A fabulously spectacular, twisting narrow road wound its way over hills and valleys, delivering scenic views by the bucketful that a camera can never capture, before eventually landing me in the mainly forgettable town of Upper Hutt, where after a short trip uphill is Kaitoke National Park: a wonderfully lush, verdant valley with camping at the equivalent of less than £3 a night. The location of the Rivendell movie set is well signposted at the small copse that was used during the filming, but as most of the scenes were digitally created and filmed on location sixteen years ago there is little to see with regards to the vistas seen in the movies. It is still a magical place, though. A peaceful evening parked alongside a bubbling stream with a small camp fire, a roast chicken and bottle of NZ's finest cheap merlot was a fine way to end the day. After ten days on the island I think I had been a bit unfair to New Zealand in my first few days; I wasn't in the right frame of mind. I had enjoyed Australia, but New Zealand has gone above it in my chart of good places to be. The climate might not be as climactic temperature-wise and summer rain is as much a fact of life as it is in Europe, but if a land is green that's because it gets wet. With hills and coastal landscapes affecting the weather, it can't help but be cooler than its global neighbour that has vast flat inland plains superheating the summer winds.

The road into Wellington was easy. The departure of the ship from the most panoramic port I have ever visited was smooth as I goggled at the views, the sea air filling my lungs and overflowing my senses as the ship entered the incredible blue fjord that leads to Picton: the 'gateway to the South Island'.

Southron Scenes – What to do when you run out of superlatives? Make some up, or would I just end up sounding a bit like Mary Poppins? Whatever the answer, I've used so many on this trip I'm at risk of sounding boring saying that the latest thing is outstanding, stupendous or fantastic, but, at the risk of being repetitive, the approach to the South Island by sea is utterly amazing! The ship cruising through Queen Charlotte Sound as it approaches the hills that surround Picton is a sight to behold, gliding through the water as the land slides by on either side of the channel.

After disembarking I followed the main two-lane road out of town over the hills towards the coast. I have made an uninformed decision to follow the east coast south, if you see what I mean, saving the recommended west coast for the trip back north, when I will also check out the mountainous region in the middle as I meander back. I want to get to Invercargill on the south coast to pay homage to Burt Monroe, *The World's Fastest Indian*. Another movie but this time based on the true story of one man with a passion for speed who set records that still stand, nearly four decades after his death.

Having made that choice of route, it's not perhaps the most stunning of the South Island scenery, but there are parts worth seeing. I've also managed a few nights' free camping in this region. There seem to be fewer restrictions although the facilities are somewhat limited, but that's fine; washing in a bucket works for me. Simple life and the compensations have been waking up to a million-dollar sea view or the peaceful surroundings of a countryside field under the shade of a tree. New Zealand's summer is a very pleasant place to be and comparable to a (good) English summer, with comfortable temperatures but always the potential for rain to keep pleasing green pastures fresh. Ying and Yang makes the world go round. So far, it seems to me that the South Island is less populated, and, like everywhere I've been in this country, getting around is not a problem even with the major roads mostly being single carriageway and limited to 100kph. It doesn't sound much (about 60mph) but with no traffic to speak of and lots to look at, what's the rush? I get a sense of the country feeling less populated and it is a pleasure to travel through. The lakes and mountains of the east coast, especially to the east of Christchurch, have an almost Scottish feel to them. A drive to the coast turned into a dirt road rally stage, the carvancamper not exactly built for this terrain, where a windswept cove with strange green-gold sand was a prelude to my arrival in Akaroa. The Scottish highland vibe was replaced by French influences in the town on the bayside with the boulangerie next to l'essence station. Sat at the side of the calm waters of the inlet, a bottle of L&P (Lemon & Paeroa) – the soft drink that is world-famous in New Zealand – and a salad baguette pass a pleasant afternoon.

Heading further south, I take a diversion inland to Fairly, which sits to the east of the Southern Alps and New Zealand's highest peak at Mount Cook. Cool mists blot out the sun and prevent a photo of the mountain, and temperatures don't rise until I reach the coast again. A visit to the steampunk HQ at Oamaru is an entertaining hour of Victorian-themed visions of future machines, as are the mysterious spherical rocks on the beach at Moeraki; the boulders formed from prehistoric rock and exhumed by tidal erosion lay on the beach. I prefer the Maori legend that they are gourds washed ashore from the wreck of the great voyaging canoe Araiteuru that brought the Maori to the South Island.

I'm not entirely sure there are any other land masses on Earth this far south other than Antarctica. Maybe the tip of South America or South Africa? Whatever the geographic truth, it is noticeably cooler at the south end of the South Island. I'm heading north again soon in search of summer, although I've run out of island, anyway!

Invercargill is, not unexpectedly, not much to write home about, but the hardware store in town sells modern tools, mechanical and service parts, general maintenance stuff. But it also doubles as an interesting museum of old vehicles, nostalgia and memorabilia, not only about Burt Munro but other kiwi motorsports legends. It's my idea of how a shop should be. It is home to the original, genuine Burt Munro special Indian Scout. A sign in the shop with words by the man himself illustrates his devotion to living his dream:

You live more in five minutes
Flat out on a bike like this than
Most people do in a lifetime

- Burt Munro

Take a 600cc bike from 1920, modified in the 1960s and
yet it still holds an unbroken land speed record today at
191mph! Let me just say that again. One hundred and ninety
one miles per hour! When you look at the bike it's hard to
imagine doing 60mph on it, never mind doing 191mph on
it! Burt Munro did that when he was in his 70s; what exactly
is stopping you from achieving anything in your life?

A night at a motor campsite just outside town is a nice
place to chill, but I wasn't expecting it in a literal sense as
waking up the next morning to 7°C was a bit of a shock
to the system, my body more acclimatised to the long
summer I have been experiencing. Time to move north,
quite literally the polar opposite of what you would do
in Europe to find warmer climes. A two-hour drive to
Queenstown saw the temperature back above 20°C; that's
better, thank you.

Queenstown is a lovely lakeside town that to me is
reminiscent of Windermere in the UK's Lake District,
which has the same backpacker, walking and water sport
themes although Queenstown is bigger, and right now
it is busy. Packed with backpackers. Haven't twenty-
somethings got anything better to do these days? Three
campsites in town are all like some European youth
refugee camp. Time to getouttatown!

With thoughts going back to my lack of superlatives,
a drive through some supercalifragilisticexpialidocious

scenery brought me to Cromwell. Although Olivier wasn't home, it does house the Highlands Motorsport Park and this weekend happens to be 'Speed Week' (sic). Guess what I'm doing this weekend? No, not just camping in the carvancamper and getting drunk on red wine. Well, yeah, I will be doing that too.

As an aside, I read Steven King's book *On Writing* and right now I'm breaking every rule in the book. But hey! Rules are meant to be broken. It's what they're for. I'm currently on my twenty-second book of this trip, *The Martian* by Andy Weir, which I guess is influencing my writing right now.

Heading north again brings me to the west coast. The fabled west coast that everyone has told me about being the place to visit on the South Island. Yeah, it's all right, I guess! If you like that sort of thing. Mountains, lakes, the odd glacier. Yeah, not much to write home about at all really. 'Scuse my French, I'm suffering from a lack of superlatives again. IT'S FUCKING AMAZING! I simply don't have the vocabulary to describe this area without resorting to over-used adjectives. Huge vistas, incredibly blue skies and vast lakes burst into vision at every turn of the road. My camera can only capture faint images that don't do it justice. I can only say if you get one chance in your life to come to New Zealand, you will not regret it. I would guarantee it, but I can't afford to refund your airfare if you are some weirdo who is not completely satisfied.

I've figured out a couple of things today as well. I've been listening to a lot of music since I've been driving rather than riding. My MP3 player has something like 4500 tracks of music so I've got plenty to go at on shuffle mode. But what it does is force me to listen to whatever is playing. All through this trip while riding the bike, I've found myself singing out loud some random tune that pops into my head, sometimes something completely obscure that I don't even like. Second but – it is freedom of thought; in the same tone, ideas, thoughts and random observations, quotes from books and song lyrics have appeared in my mind. Listening to my music has filtered, masked and blocked those random brainwaves. I switched the music off today, wound all the windows down and blew away the cobwebs in my mind. The other thing was that driving is not very interactive. It probably is, but it's less interactive with the immediate surroundings than riding a bike. I'm sat in a comfortable chair. I can control the environmental surroundings with more/less wind/air/ heat/cool. A bad/wet road surface doesn't matter. I can choose in-car entertainment. I can sit back, relax and take as much or as little notice of the passing world as I choose. If only more car drivers experienced just once the utter involvement in riding a bike, its complete connection with its surroundings and the rider's total control required to make it all happen. If you've never done it, I can't explain the difference any clearer than choose life – choose a bike!

When we live in crowded cities surrounded by the constant noise of modern life, competing for power, money and material things, we lose sight of the real world. Perhaps that's how we stay sane in the madness of it all. Opening your eyes and seeing the complex beauty of the natural wonders of the world is a wonderful, life-enhancing experience.

A song of mountains and ice – continuing the slightly Scottish theme of the South Island's highlands, I camped at a site in Bannockburn, so utterly quiet and dark at night that I could only hear the ticking of my own heartbeat or the voices of the Germans that, despite having a whole field to camp in, decide to park right next to me. Just a ten-minute drive down the road is Cromwell, where the Highlands Motorsport Park is situated. A modern development that has everything a motorsport park should, including an interesting museum with historic race cars, bikes and stories of famous New Zealand racers. Sitting on a grassy bank in the summer sun with a cool beer, accompanied by the rumble of V8 engines competing with more nimble old British sports cars around the complex twists and turns of the circuit, is a sense of '60s cool under the summer sun. The most amazing car shape ever built to my uneducated eye – a two-door '57 Chevrolet Bel Air – was among the many interesting old motors on display, all set to the backdrop of mountains and clear blue skies. The owner is an expat Scottish pet food millionaire and retired car racer and I can full understand why he bought and developed his own petrolhead playground in such an amazing scenic location.

I am feeling slightly inadequate now, though, as one vehicle on display was a 1981 Ford tractor that had travelled around the world towing a caravan. A tractor! With a sign indicating a max speed of 20kph it only took a year to complete the journey. I've met cyclists, I've met walkers, I've met car drivers in totally inappropriate cars taking their own version of an overland adventure. I didn't expect anyone to have done it on a tractor!

Back at the campsite and parked up in a slightly different spot to catch the evening sun, new campers arrive and park a discreet distance away, followed by the returning Germans who park between us. Do they get lonely, I wonder?

I've also got a bit of sunburn after the day at the races. The sun seems especially hot in New Zealand. All through the trip I've been careful to avoid being burnt and by now I've stopped worrying about getting too much sun as my skin is tanned enough to be able to deal with some hot sunshine, but this far south the ozone is thin and sunburn a real risk. My lack of attention to sun protection pays me back.

Heading north-west from Wanaka, the lakes and scenery expand and explode into view with an intensity that is impossible to describe. At a narrow point of land called The Neck, the road crosses from the western shore of Lake Hawea to the eastern shore of Lake Wanaka, where I have to take a pause just to say wow! You think you've seen the most amazing view ever, only for it to be outdone at the next turn of the road or crest of the hill. It would be easy to become blasé when your vision is overloaded with so much input, but, honestly, every single sight takes your breath away. As the valley narrows, the river becomes fast-flowing white water over numerous waterfalls, cascading over rocks until it levels out and the water meanders through wide gravel beds, leading to an open flat plain bisected by a wide riverbed at Haast. It's a superb biking road and, judging by the numbers, many bikers of all denominations seemed to be in agreement. I stopped so many times that a little 1920s Austin 7 pick-up truck kept passing me as it trundled along the same route at a steady pace: the Austin tortoise and the Toyota hare. Once I got to the coast, huge distances of tropical rainforest followed, punctuated by clear lake waters or the sweeping beaches seemingly untouched by humans. Sand blasted, wave-tossed and sunbleached tree trunks holding all the land rights on the grey sand.

At Fox Glacier I took a two-night stop to have a day free so I could have a close-up look at the blue ice of the glacier. I had a slight 'is that it?' moment after hiking up to the viewing point; there's lots of gravel at the foot of the ice flow, its retreat along the valley seemingly unstoppable as the water drains ceaselessly down the impressively vast ice-carved valley. The price of progress elsewhere on this little planet.

It's late lunchtime and a cafe on the main street has tasty food, a cool beer and a backpacking ukulele player sat quietly strumming on the street corner, providing a gentle backdrop to accompany the chirping cicadas, the tranquillity almost constantly broken by the frequent thud of helicopter blades ferrying those with the credit card balance to see the prettier side of the glacier, thereby adding to the problem that is reducing the glacier. The issue of hot sun again making its presence known as I feel it burning my tanned skin as I sit on the café's veranda. I find shade sat next to the carvancamper and take comfort in a bottle of beer from the supermarket across the road. A little further north the day after, the same echoing peace is utterly undisturbed, the tourists' helicopter flights concentrating on ice flows rather than the simple natural beauty of the forested mountains and lakes. A small flightless bird hoots, cicadas chirp, all under the ever-present watch of the ancient wooded hills as a swim in the cool, still waters of a lake eases my prickling sunburn.

What is it with Germans? All through New Zealand, there are lots of them; here, back in Cromwell, the German couple seemed intent on being my near neighbours. I don't have a problem with Germans as such, but in a DOC (department of conservation) campsite there is lots of space, a whole field. Yet they park next to me. At an empty car park with a fabulous view of the mountains I stop to make a cup of tea. A bloody great rented campervan rolls up next to me, blotting out the view, followed by a cheery "Hallo" in a German accent. At a campsite that is fairly busy, the site owner says park anywhere, so I find one section where there's no one else (it's furthest away from the toilet block!). Late in the evening a campervan rolls in and parks right next to me. You can guess the spoken language!

When I was young(er) the phrase 'at the turn of the century' referred to the 1900s and 'historical' referred to some artefact or location. It occurred to me today that the same phrase now refers to the year 2000. I must be getting old! I raise the subject because New Zealand, like most countries, offers tourist guidance via a brown-coloured signpost for points of significant interest. In the UK that often refers to a medieval castle or ruined abbey. New Zealand's 'historical' sites are from the 'old' turn of the century, often a World War Two site or post-1900 event. A lot like Australia, there is very little indication that there was civilisation prior to the European invasion, but at least New Zealand seems to acknowledge the Maori culture a lot better than Australia does the Aboriginal.

Further north, I turned inland as the coastal route was getting a bit less interesting. The mountains might be gentler than the Southern Alps, but the scenery, flora and fauna are just as incredible as ever. An overnight stop at a DOC site on the shores of a deep, dark water lake provides another chance to swim into the evening, but biting flies force me to retreat into the carcancamper and I'm asleep by 8pm. The next morning's early start gives an opportunity to cover some miles. New Zealand has a lot of narrow, single-carriageway bridges and Give Way signs at each end ensure the infrequent traffic arranges its own passage according to the oncoming traffic. Not difficult when the number of vehicles on the road is as low as it is. However, my experience of the day was one particular single-track bridge that is also the crossing point for the railway line! That fact brings a whole new meaning to the perspective of 'GIVE WAY'.

Summer, sea and sand dunes – You probably need to be listening to The Doors – *The End* – while reading this, as camping in the peace and quiet with time and space is once again giving my mind time to wander. Have you ever sat under a clear night sky and utterly marvelled at the unthinkable vastness of visible space before you? The stars and planets visible to the naked eye, a mere fraction of what there is of the known universe. And how totally and completely insignificant you are in this huge theatre of light. All of life's worries and everything that brings concern to your everyday 'blink of an eye' existence all boil down to an improbable collection of chemical elements. Stop worrying about anything; in the end it absolutely doesn't matter!

In other philosophical news, England's claim to be a green and pleasant land is way off beam. The description is far more fitting of New Zealand. I'm sorry, I realise my enthusiasm for these islands must be slightly wearing now, but I'm finding it difficult to understand why more people just don't live here, simple as that, I guess. Being fortunate enough to have been born in England, I have been blind to a wider view of the world. It seems from afar that England and Europe are in a mess. My view has widened immeasurably during my travels. A few stats I have looked up put things into perspective for me:

UK land mass 241,590 sq km
NZ land mass 268,021 sq km

11% bigger than the UK

NZ population 4.37 million
UK population 63.18 million

Fourteen times more than New Zealand

Meanwhile, back in NZ, summer is in full bloom and hot, sunny, lazy days are relaxing and easy. I will miss summer; it's been ten months long this year. Driving further north, I pass through Wakefield, Foxhill and Dovedale and past Whitby Bay until I reach Nelson, where I happened on a plain-fronted building with a simple sign that said 'NZ

Classic Motorcycles'. I wasn't sure if it was a shop or a business, but I pulled in to investigate. I was very glad I did as it is an amazing (private) collection of old motorcycles from the 1920s through to more modern machines. There are lots of 1950s and 1960s Triumphs, Nortons, BSAs, Indians, Harleys and others I didn't recognise. Three amazing Brough Superiors and a Britten, wow! I'm in motorcycle heaven!

After two nights at a campsite quirkily named Quinney's Bush that turned out to be popular with families filling the public holiday weekend, I moved on. From somewhere full of thirty-somethings with young kids, along with the grandparents, to a less facilitated campsite full of twenty-somethings avoiding responsibility. Not quite sure where I fit into that grand scheme of things. Perhaps I don't and that's the whole point. Sat on a pebble sea break with a turquoise sea in front of me and misty mountains on the horizon, I'm not sure there is much more. A bed to sleep in, a bottle of cheap wine, I think I'm turning into a bit of a hippy; peace, man!

Heading towards the north-west point of the South Island, I make a brief stop at the (very busy) beautiful bay at Kaiteriteri, where bathers swim the shallow waters between rocky islands. I cross the mountain road at Abel Tasman National Park, to Collingwood which is a fantastic place, wonderful scenery... Yeah, I know, you've heard it all before, but really, a truly stunning area to be in. Twisting mountainous roads, jaw-dropping views and today, picture perfect weather to enjoy it all. At the north western tip there's a spit of land jutting 24km out into the sea. Farewell Spit is a huge bar of rolling sand dunes with open ocean on one side and the tidal Golden Bay on the other. A fantastic and hugely interesting place, with sweeping hills running down to steep cliffs and a wide, clean beach in front of rolling sand dunes on the seaward side. I read that a lot of whale strandings occur on that beach due to the huge tide that leaves shallow sand banks for miles. Luckily, the tide was in when I visited so the sea was right up to the base of the dunes. On my way back, a diversion takes me to Wharaiki beach, which after a bit of hike provided more stunning sand dunes and a scenic beach to take a cooling dip.

Camping by a fast-flowing tidal estuary at Mapua saw out the hot final weekend on the South Island. Saturday was a fabulous day covering an unplanned near-50km on a rented bicycle along a cycle route through and around the oddly named Rabbit Island (not a single oryctolagus cuniculus to be seen) and out to the little coastal town of Richmond near the 'City of Nelson'. With the tide having filled the estuary, cooling down with a swim in clear blue water on the way back was fabulous. After taking too long on my leisurely ride back I only just made it in time to catch the last ferry of the day across the estuary, the boat's pilot explaining to me how he gave up a career in the UK after graduating from Sheffield University to move to New Zealand, where ferrying passengers pays no money but the quality of life is lovely. What a cool thing to do. The 15% discount card from the cycle hire business for the cafe across the road ensured I replaced the calories I had managed to burn off!

I chose to take the scenic coastal road back to Picton; why wouldn't you? Through the 'green mussel capital' of Havelock, with enormous views of the water and surrounding hills, it put 'scenic' into the next dimension (again). News reports of an earthquake in Christchurch reminded me that these islands are 'alive' in so many ways. No casualties, and no tremors made it this far north. After a night at a motor camp just outside town, the journey on the 9am ferry north passed quickly as I chatted to an early retired couple returning from a walking holiday/break to the wilds of the South Island.

Quickly out of Wellington and on my way north, I passed the Kaitoke National Park (waving to the elven folk at Rivendell) where I had stopped on my way south, driving through Masterson to end up at a beautiful little riverside campsite in 'kiwi country' at Eketahuna. Despite keeping my eyes peeled for the little flightless burrow dwellers, just like the rabbits at Mapua, none made an appearance.

Following the coastal road north west through Hastings, I stopped at the 'art deco'-designed town of Napier, which was rebuilt after a 1920s earthquake. A gathering of 1930s cars outside the 'Gatsby'-themed hotel added to the ambience.

Looking at a map suggested an overland route that had camping around a large inland lake, but half an hour along the road I spotted a sign that said there was 105km of unpaved road after the lake. Not wanting to subject the carvancamper to a road more suitable to four-wheel-drive vehicles, I turned around and found an overnight rest at a riverside campsite behind a tea shop in Morere. Famous for its hot springs, it was peaceful and warm overnight, although it's late summer now and you can tell. The mornings are cooler as the southern hemisphere heads towards autumn, but the days are still very apt to warm up quickly. I had a sudden strange thought (while not staring at the stars this time) that I am actually upside down! The gravity of that situation struck me as funny! Following the spectacular road to Gisborne brought me to the Waioeka Gorge. (Pronounce it how you like, I don't know!) Although the day turned rainy, the low cloud hanging in the trees and hills brought a mystical edge to the region as the road swooped and turned its way following the contours of the river for the length of the narrow channel carved into the scenery. An amazing road to drive along through misty mountains, the river waters flowing like a timeless craftsman, carving the valley. Native bush flora with huge ferns and amazing trees allowed this traveller the occasional glimpse of rushing high-rise waterfalls tumbling down the sheer cliffs. As the road reached the coast at Whakatane (wh pronounced f, cue schoolboy humour) the Pacific storm wind strengthened and the rain lashed as I stopped overnight on my route back to Paereo for the weekend's motorbike races. Assuming the storm passes over.

Paeroa (pronounced pie rower) is the 'P' in L&P. I hadn't realised that in my time in New Zealand. I know that doesn't mean much to anyone in the UK, but the 'lemony' soft drink is the popular bottled fizz in NZ. 'World Famous in New Zealand since ages ago', it was originally made by combining lemon juice with carbonated mineral water from the town. Paeroa is also (almost) famous for its motorcycle street race and that's what I'm here for. Before the races, though, Saturday was put over to a car and bike show with an eclectic mix of old and new, interesting and downright strange! '50s cool street rods, modern restorods and custom cars of all designs sharing the racecourse field with restored '60s bikes, café racers, street fighters and a multitude of Harleys, all on the site I had camped at on my first night in New Zealand. After wandering around the show and watching the motors parade through the town, I stopped at the wonderful Karangahake Reserve on the way back to the campsite I had landed at just outside town. Old mine workings along a narrow river gorge have become a leisurely walk. Tramlines still go through dark tunnels with 'windows' out to the gorge. No lighting or signs means stepping into the inky blackness on trust that 'it must be this way'. Luckily, I was right and I didn't fall into an unseen abyss. A wobbly suspension bridge and a walkway cut into the cliff brought me back to my starting point. What a fabulous little place!

'Battle of the streets' – Sunday's Paeroa street races were entertainment on a level that I completely identify with. Modern and classic bikes, young guys out to prove their lack of fear and old hands still giving it back. Outgunned old stagers still sliding tyres wildly to the edge of the hay bales lined up against the street furniture. Raucous open-piped Triumphs and Nortons, a couple of Ducatis and Moto Guzzi in the BEARs (British European and American racing) race. There are races for the latest superbikes and other races for supermotos and then bikes that looked like they belonged in a museum. All doing what they were designed to do well in their respective era: going as fast as the human on board dare go! All within touching distance of the viewing public. With no visible

196

police presence, it was left to the exiting crowds to organise themselves at the road junctions, but it didn't seem to be a problem. It's a smaller crowd than a world championship event, granted, but traffic has a way of finding its own way. Some organisations would do well to remember that!

Take cover! – One sound that will resonate in my memory of New Zealand is the haunting wail of a World War Two air raid siren. Used to call the volunteer fire service into action, it's a sound that carries across the hills and even for me, despite not being old enough to have experienced the fear that echoing drone must have brought, it is a sound that triggers childhood dread from an age when cold wars were new. While I think about day-to-day experiences of life in New Zealand, the currency confusion is one thing that's puzzled me since I've been here. The smallest coin they have is 10 cents and there are 100 cents to a dollar. So why are items sold at less than fractions of 10¢? If a shopping total comes to $25.73, for example, they give you change to the nearest 10¢, which is a bloody silly idea!

This wanderer is not lost – the movie set of Hobbiton is the home of the Bagginses' brought to life. It might be make-believe, but it's more real than any theme park fantasy, with more moral meanings in the stories that we could do a lot worse than to live by. It's a shame the tour is so organised. It would be great to be able to wander freely about the site, viewing the hobbit holes and marvelling at the attention to detail, while trying to spot the fake plants and trees from the real thing. Instead, it is a guided tour, with groups led to each location as the tour guide gives a talk about the point of interest. An ale in the Green Dragon looking out over the lake at the end of the tour is a fine way to spend some time. It also eased the shock at the prices in that gift shop on the way out; thanks, but no thanks. It is still a great experience to visit if you're ever in this part of the world. Just don't buy a replica sword.

A few days by the coast back in the Bay of Plenty will see out my last bit of time in New Zealand. The carvancamper is due for return to Auckland and I move on, always moving on, but this time somewhat reluctantly. At the campsite I have sorted out flight bookings and spent some time sorting out the carvancamper for its return, packing what I will need in some sort of order, with the important stuff at the top of my bag. I've also spent a lot of time contemplating where I am, where I've been and where I'm going next. The USA has never held much fascination for me; I don't want the big city experience. I would happily stay exactly where I am, if only it were that simple.

Back in Auckland, a hotel not too far from the airport is my final port of call in what has been a wonderful time in New Zealand. Sat looking at the busy city outside the hotel, it somehow seems a world away from the rest of the country. I have always been really bad at going home from any adventure, holiday, weekend away or even a day trip. I love travelling, and going home at the end always seems an anti-climax. I had wondered when I started out on this journey if I would feel the same at the end. If after so long away from home I would actually look forward to going home, back to familiarity, back to what I know and where I'm from. The truth is I'm not. I am reluctant to leave here, to move on again this time, on what is the last leg of my trip. I could keep doing what I have done since April last year for the rest of my life and be happy with that life, but in a positive moment it isn't the end yet. There is still a whole continent to visit, to get a glimpse of in the short time I have left. That may be enough, given my thoughts on visiting the USofA; it may ignite my ambition to see more of it. I guess I'll find out.

16 USA ARIZONA – TIME TO FIRE UP THE FLUX CAPACITOR

Time Travelling Man – After bidding a sad farewell to New Zealand it's time to move on again. Although it's not a DeLorean, a Boeing 777 leaves at a quarter to eight in the evening and carries me on the twelve-and-a-half-hour flight to San Francisco. My flight departs SF three hours after that before an hour-and-a-half flight to Phoenix, Arizona. About seventeen hours' travel time and I arrive at the motel in Phoenix two hours before I left Auckland on the same day. I've got a day back of my life. Time travel is a reality!

Hello, America – San Francisco, whatever day it is, or was. I'm not wearing flowers in my hair and didn't get to meet any particularly gentle people either. Just passing through, man! Phoenix, Arizona. Cacti, warning signs for snakes: this is cowboy country. Bike riders are 90% Harley or Victory-mounted, cowboy boots, denim waistcoat and no crash helmet is the order of the day, it seems. Not sure how much protection a bandana provides. Enough to look cool, I guess.

Driving out of the valley in my rented Korean-built Chevy Trax, the road rises from the valley floor, where Phoenix bakes in the early spring sunshine, into the cooler mountains. Fir trees line the badly surfaced road and snow still clings to the banking. It was early autumn the day before yesterday. I've skipped winter this year. The measurements have gone back in time too. Miles I'm used to in confused Britain that mixes metric and imperial. But fuel is by the gallon, fruit is sold by the pound, liquid by the quart and temperature in Fahrenheit. I hadn't realised how much I accept metric measurements, until there are none. While we're on the subject, one US gallon equals 3.785 litres. Filling up at $1.79 a gallon, which I work out to be roughly 33p per litre. Hmmm! No wonder there are so many HUGE monster pick-up trucks around with V8 motors measured in cubic inches.

At 7000 feet altitude (that's 2130 metres), Flagstaff will be my base camp for a couple of days. I'm right on Route 66; a quick view of the Grand Canyon is an easy drive from here and Monument Valley is not too far to travel before I move on to seek out some iconic Route 66 memorabilia. I'm into US tourist mode, doing one sight and moving on to the next. Hot damn!

Holes in the ground – The Grand Canyon is an iconic symbol of America, but, unlike lots of icons, it lived up to its billing. More than lived up to it! I was genuinely stunned by the scale and immense natural beauty of this wonder of the world. The layers distinctly highlighting what geologists see in lumps of rock. Getting away from the built-up visitor facilities shows the area at its natural best and as usual I appreciated being away from other human beings, especially when they are excitable 'jeewudchalookatit' Americans!

A bit further down the road is a meteor crater showing what the impact of a small rock can be, given enough velocity. The information at the site says the crater is 1200m diameter and suggests the meteor was approximately 50m and the speed of impact 12.8km/second (28,000mph), with an impact of about ten megatons. The meteorite was mostly vaporised on impact about 50,000 years ago: quite an amazing sight.

Route 66 – the 'mother road', 'America's High Street', all the other clichés that apply. In reality, Route 66 is little more than a collection of towns along the remains of the old highway to California, surviving by means of memorabilia and tourists keen to live the legend. The modern Interstate 40 allows free-flowing modern traffic to bypass once-thriving businesses, but the romanticism of the migration of the population from the recession-hit east to the golden west coast, along a road bridging the continent, continues to draw travellers to the dusty remains. There is something that makes it worthwhile, a vision of what was, an escape route to a better life. The human belief of being in control of our own destiny is as bright today as it was a hundred years ago.

I got as far as Seligman, where the dusty remains of what once was linger on in the twenty-first century. Angel's Barber Shop in the town was once a barber's shop, but like the rest of the town the owner has passed away and it has become a tourist gift shop. An evening stop 40 miles west, in the little town of Williams, is a cool place to rest for the night. A motel room with a porch allows me to give neighbourly nods to fellow travellers as I take a cool beer until the sun goes down.

'GET BACK' – **The Beatles**

Tucson, Arizona – after the cool 62°F Ponderosa pine-covered mountain town of Flagstaff, modern Tucson is a hot, sprawling mass of low-rise buildings, filling the flat valley floor as far as the eye can see, surrounded by a low mountain range heavily populated with enormous cacti, and it's sweltering under the 90°F midday sun. The motel is cheap and nasty, without the cheap, and from a vantage point on Sentinel Peak the view is less than appealing. Arizona is where summer spends the winter and hell spends the summer, according to the information boards in town.

Standing on a corner in Winslow, Arizona, and I'm quite sure I'm in the wrong song. The apparent misspelling of Tucson is explained on an information board, in the Native American Tohono O'odham language: Tyuk-son. Tyuk meaning 'black spring' and son for the 'foot of a hill'. So it's not the Koreans that got it wrong with the Hyundai Tucson! So 'Too-sohn', not much to write home about really. However! Just outside town in a valley wonderfully blessed with iconic desert scenery is Old Tucson, a western town used as a movie set for many cowboy films and TV series including *Rio Bravo*, *The Outlaw Jose Wales* and *Tombstone*. The dusty street, the boardwalk storefronts and saloon, the town hall, sheriff's office and every other clichéd western scene is here. All have been walked in by people like John Wayne and Clint Eastwood. There are staged gunfights, informational demonstrations and shops selling native Indian and related gifts. The buildings are complete and not just fake-fronted props. I get roped into a street-side demonstration show that is a pastiche of the old west quack-doctors-cure-all potions. Failing to hit a drum on cue earns me a bottle of meadowsweet-flavoured root beer that has a common ingredient with the cure-all medicinal cream from my childhood and tastes like Germolene smells. It is strangely nice!

Wandering into the desert later, the size of the cacti have to be seen to be believed at well over three times my modest two-metre height! With desert plants, cacti of all shapes, small lizards and probably lots of snakes, this of the real wild west and away from the sprawling modernity of twenty-first-century Arizona, the real country is still alive, well and probably unchanged since the native American tribes wandered this land. I read an article in a local magazine about Arizona and in it was a section about water shortages. It stated that there is just the right amount of water in the desert; the problems start when people decide to build a city in it!

Back in Phoenix, a really, really cheap and particularly nasty motel near the airport is my last night. Arizona has been an interesting place to visit and getting away from the crowds is easy. Monument Valley wasn't achievable due to not being allowed to take a rented car onto the dirt track through the Native American land, but everything else was well worth seeing and I will actually be sad to return my little Chevy back to the airport car hire centre. Winter is coming – this will be my last glimpse of this eleven-month-long summer. After Arizona's warm sunshine it's time to head to the chill of March in more northerly latitudes. Best dig out the extra clothes I've carried just for that occasion. Hopefully, by the time I get back to England the winter will have eased its icy grey fingers and signs of early spring will be in the air. I can only hope!

17 USA NEW YORK STATE – THE WINDS OF WINTER

Americans, a generalisation: it's nothing personal, but really!? I've experienced lots of cultures on this trip and maybe my own opinion is affecting my view, but why are they all so GODDAMN LOUD?! Airport announcements I can kinda understand need to be, but they are delivered in a high-pitched female wail like she's on amphetamines. S-l-o-w down and people might just have a chance of understanding you, love! In a taco bar, one guy complains because he doesn't like what he's ordered, spoken at a volume just so everyone sitting at the tables can hear. I guess you just picked the wrong item off the menu. Shouting at the poor girl at the cash till won't help. The false over-excitable positivity is positively wearing. A teenage girl says to a uniformed soldier, "Thanks for your service." Now, while that is a worthy statement, it just comes across as overly false to me. It says thank God we're all safe in the world because of the US army! I've overheard so many 'private' conversations, both between two people talking face-to-face or like one guy on the phone, all held at a volume so that everyone can hear. The guy on the phone actually looking around the bus I was on as he spoke, just checking everyone is listening to how important he is. Subtlty is lost on them, it seems. 'God bless 'Merica (y'all').

In a New York minute – After eleven months of summer it's bloody freezing back in the northern hemisphere. At -2°F winter is lingering and icy patches of dirty snow line the sidewalk. Getting outta town was my primary target on arrival at JFK. Queens, Brooklyn, the Bronx: all names that have conjured up images of New York in a mostly less than luminous light. It's not a pretty place for the most part, lots of streets under the constant shadow of the steel support for the overhead train lines. Clichéd steam venting from the grates in the road, yellow cabs with no English-speaking drivers, finding their way by satellite, everyone preoccupied with their own little bubble of existence, not wanting to encourage conversation or even interest. The world is so much more open outside of this large metropolis, where globally it seems to me that the self-centred, the self-important and those driven by opportunity, money or ambitions of power seem to gather in their millions.

'AMERICAN LAND' – **Bruce Springsteen**

It's an old story. – 'Where the streets are paved with gold' – and it's still being played out today at the channel ports, the Mexican border and in the Mediterranean. Give me the open smile and interested conversation of someone who sees beauty in open spaces and blues skies. Those are the real human beings. Those are the people who can see the world for what it is and not the dumping ground of human waste that so much of our planet has become.

On a lighter note! Driving out of New York City in my rented Nee-Sahn with CVT transmission that cost me $10 to fill with petrol, up to the Catskill region in upstate New York is a very nice area to be. The Hudson valley hugging the wide waters of the Hudson River. Classical old-style wooden houses clustered around small towns, and huge bridges spanning the cold waters. No sign of leaves on the trees, but the weather forecast is for milder temperatures; in fact, the forecast says record temperatures for the time of year.

My long, hot summer has come to an abrupt end, but it was amazing while it lasted. The days are clear, crisp and actually beautiful in their own way. Winter is on the wane, but from what I have seen so far there's little in the way of signs of spring in the slow-to-react flora. The trees still have naked branches and the grass around so many of the houses is brown and obviously recovering from the harshness of the northern winter.

Just another American observation: drive-through burger joints; okay, I can understand that. I've seen drive-through beer sales in Australia, but a drive-through ATM has to be the ultimate in car culture laziness.

1969 Aquarian Exposition – Peace and love, man! There are lots of 'kills' around here. Murderkill River, Broadkill and Whorekill Rivers, also Catskill, Peeskill, Fishkill. The list goes on. Less entertaining than the names is the explanation. A body of water, a kill, is a creek, the word coming from the Dutch kille, meaning riverbed or water channel, and seeing as the Dutch were the first Europeans to settle the area it makes more sense. So now you know! Also Leeds and Stockport. Chelsea and New Hamburg, to name only a few. Places that didn't grow to the same proportions as New York, but nevertheless originated from the Europeans who moved to the new world. Globally there has been a common theme of Europeans 'discovering' and occupying new countries. I wonder how different our world would be had native peoples fought off the white invaders.

A trip up towards the Catskill Mountains brought me to a couple of places that live according to the '60s hippie mantra (man) of peace and love and music and whatever else sells to bring in the visiting tourist. New Paltz is a small town on a hillside with a meandering brown tributary of the Hudson River flowing at the base of the main street. There are significant Irish influences, with a couple of Irish-themed pubs and the shamrock in evidence in most places, only outdone by the number of peace symbols. Given my earlier thoughts about the American way and the 'thanks for your service' speech to a uniformed soldier, I wonder how the 'peace' thing sits with the American conscience. I've read lots about that era and the friction between the factions. I guess that issue still sits there under the bubble of the 'World Police' psyche.

Woodstock – THE gig to be at as 1969 drew to a close. Unfortunately, I was only six years old at the time! But the spirit of the age lives on in the sleepy little town nearest to the venue of the last big hippie event of the '60s. A few of the local inhabitants, it seems, are clinging onto the event. An old guy in flared and patched rainbow dungarees wanders around the town singing at the top of his voice to accompany a barefoot chap playing the didgeridoo while sat on the benches in the centre of the village, his long, matted grey beard reaching his chest and, seemingly, his befuddled brain still seeking inner equilibrium. Later on I see him walking hand in hand with a younger girl. Maybe it's just an act to entertain the visitors. Tie-dye clothing, art, music and cafes all cater for the visitor seeking enlightenment from the heady days of the peace movement. Empty shops and for sale signs indicate that maybe business isn't always what it should be in the sleepy corner of upstate New York.

A sign proclaims:

'On this site stood a local market bankrupted by the monopolistic, make-it-cheaper-in China, anti-union big box store where you shop'

Hudson Valley – The wide, deep waters of the Hudson River are surrounded on both banks by heavily wooded country. At this time of year these trees are leafless, but I imagine during the summer and probably especially in autumn the scenery would be amazingly colourful. The towns and villages in the area do look to have been hit quite hard by the financial crash. Huge shopping malls have lots of empty lots; there are 'abandoned' business premises all over the place. I guess the cost of living outweighs the cost of a steak, especially when you get a side order of fries and everything that goes with it. Judging by the typical size, most people seem to have done just that!

I've seen lots of TV series about buying and restoring old cars in the USA, and looking around it does seem that there are lots of old vehicles sat slowly decaying among the woodpile next to barns and houses. This far north, salted roads are a winter fact, with the subsequent corrosion issues for the local cars, but rusted sills, it seems, are not a roadworthiness issue in New York State. Given the nationalistic stance of most Americans, I have been surprised by the number of Japanese vehicles. It's true there are lots of Chevrolets and Jeeps and the HUGE GMC and Ford F150 pick-up trucks and Sport Utillidy ve-hickles are mostly US-branded (even if some of them are built in Korea), but they seem to be greatly outnumbered by foreign cars. In fact, looking back around the whole journey, Japanese cars have a huge presence all over the world. I'm just surprised that the average Joe in stars 'n' stripes allows his wallet to override his sense of national duty! Then again, I guess price, reliability and equipment will override nationalistic beliefs when the buck in your wallet buys less.

Up into the Catskill Mountains a huge silence hangs in the trees. Driving through Pheonicia and out into the hills, there is an overpowering sense of stillness and, strangely, I don't even hear the sound of bird calls. With ice still lingering on a pond, the silence is broken by the sound of a falling tree somewhere on the hillside and then by a Subaru roaring past with the exhaust pipe only just hanging from its tail end. Modern life just won't stay out of the way. A twisting road passes a famous waterfall, but it was impossible to get close to on foot. I guess if it was a drive-through it would be accessible. Apparently, nineteenth-century painters and writers flocked to the area, but the 'view' was nowhere near anything envisioned in an old painting by Asher Brown Durand called Kindred Spirits. Painted in 1849, it shows two men standing on a rock ledge in the Catskills in a lost world setting that looks as if it would take an expedition to reach. Below them in a shadowy chasm, a stream dashes through a jumble of boulders and beyond, glimpsed through the canopy of leaves, is a long, gorgeously forbidding view of the mountains and ranks of trees that vanish into darkness. It is so untamed and full of the impenetrable beyond; you would die out there. Nothing like that exists now, just another road bridging the river. Perhaps it never did and it was simply artistic licence. This is also the land of Rip Van Winkle. Sleepy old man! I think sleeping out the travel through America might have been a nice idea!

The actual town of Catskill is standard fare again for these New York state towns, which have that slightly down-at-heel feel. A main street with lots of empty stores, peeling paint on the wooden-built houses. Groups of unemployed men watching the world go by. I've tried not to be 'down' on the USA, but it's obvious to me that there are lots of issues with loss of business and industry. In huge contrast, the little town of Highland Falls is an image of affluence. New cars parked on the streets and several franchised dealer shops stacked with stocks of big trucks, shiny cars and American motorcycles. The reason? The town is also home to West Point, the US military academy. The war machine obviously pays well.

I get back to the ever-present still waters of the Hudson River, and, with the temperatures warming up, the number of people sitting by the water's edge increases as the afternoon sun brings a feeling of spring.

18 LONDON – BACK IN BLIGHTY

'STREETS OF LONDON' – **Ralph McTell**

A short Atlantic hop. It's not over, but it's close. London calling, just another big city to get out of ASAP and hopefully be reunited with my trusty motorbike. I've missed my faithful travel partner. Sending it home from Australia was absolutely the right thing to do, but my journey has been lessened without it. I became just another tourist, just another rental car on the road, anonymous as a world traveller. The bike parked at fuel stations, cafes, campsites and hotels was always a topic of conversation, always a source of wonder at the sense of adventure and an illustration of the journey. I am very sad to say that this HUGE adventure is in its closing stages. I can't begin to imagine how I'm going to cope with going back to my normal life or work and the fact of not travelling onwards continually. That, I guess, is something I will have to come to terms with. I didn't set out on this journey looking for answers to unknown questions and, consequently, I haven't found any. I have, though, generated a few questions about my own life and where I go from here. With the sights and experiences I have had over the last twelve months, I think my perspective has been irrevocably altered.

You are not what you own – all the trivial things that tie us down, the obsession with personal belongings and the unimportant things that gain a higher-than-deserved level of our attention. The things that stop us from exploring everything the world has to offer and bring our focus into a narrow margin instead of raising our eyes and seeing the world for what it is and not what is reported as being. There are lots of fabulous, amazing and wonderful experiences to grasp hold of. Switch off the news and find your own answers; they are not in the biased views of the news reports that attempt to bring a sense of community where it is divided by cultural differences and political opinions. Different people see things differently; that is inherently human. Trying to pretend we are all the same is not going to work. Russians wholeheartedly believe their own country is stronger and safer than any other; so do Koreans and Australians. New Zealand is! Local news gives a local bias to its reports and the UK is no different. The BBC is no less biased on its reporting than the Russian news agency.

London standing on a damp platform waiting for a late train – it's a bank holiday, it's raining and it's windy and grey. There is obvious security at Heathrow; trains are delayed or cancelled due to bad weather. It's England at the end of March, not much changes. After an overnight flight via Dublin on Aer Lingus, I end up in a hotel near the shipping agent's and my bike is available for collection on Tuesday. It might just be a damp ride north.

After a full English breakfast in the conservatory of the hotel looking at the sun shining on the River Thames it doesn't feel so bad. My bike is mostly as I left it. A few extra dings, a couple of extra scratches. The crate arrived damaged and it looks like it's been on its side at some point, but it's nothing too dramatic. After putting the front wheel back on and screwing the mirrors and screen in place, it started first time. The battery had not been disconnected but was still fully charged; the engine oil was at minimum, though. I wonder if that is another indication of it not being upright for the duration of its journey. The tyres were low on air but other than that, it is just the signs of long travel that are evident, and I love the used patina of the bike now.

Getting out of London, the sense of crowds is huge; the feeling of people everywhere is overwhelming. The M25 is busy, the traffic slowed by constant 50mph variable speed limits. Cameras are everywhere, monitoring every vehicle's speed through the automatic fine collection points. No one cares that my bike is returning from a huge adventure; no one notices the travel stickers. Everyone seems to be self-obsessed and it feels like I need a neon sign pointing out what I've achieved. But instead; I'm anonymous. Just another bike on the road. Just another bloke who obviously can't afford to run a car.

The weather is kind and cool spring sunshine accompanies me on my journey north. Arrival at home is less appealing. It's not a place that makes me happy but there's nowhere else to go, no moving on to something new. Just back to the real world. A lack of adventure and a loss of freedom.

Things need to change. This is my next challenge.

19 FINAL DESTINATION

'LONGTIME' – **Boston**

To be back in a cold, over-populated world filled with its own self-importance is a shock to the system. Where money and status is all that matters and England's reputation as a green and pleasant land has seemingly been lost in the fog of progress. I think about what I've achieved and what worked and what didn't!

The bike – I was unsure if a genial commuter bike would stand up to the journey I planned. It was and is no accepted vision of an adventure motorcycle as sold by the established purveyors of packaged overland motorcycles like BMW or KTM. But I believe any bike you have an adventure on qualifies as an 'adventure motorcycle'. Another major qualification for a bike on an adventure is to be reliable, which it was, completely. The only issues were a bit of overheating in Siberia after liberally coating the radiator with a mixture of clay, diesel and wet sand. The temperature warning light came on again heading south into the Australian outback in 40°C heat. My own internal temperature warning light was glowing brightly at the time too! A failed rear wheel bearing was replaced with the aid of a brick as a makeshift hammer drifting out the bearing with a socket extension! One replacement set of brake pads and a chain and sprockets were also fitted while I was in Australia. After the harshness of crossing Kazakhstan and Siberia, the short list of mechanical maladies is a tribute to the tough little Versys.

Suspension – upgrading the bike's suspension prior to setting off was a hugely successful, albeit slightly expensive modification that was worth every penny. Properly equipped, the bike floated over rough tarmac, coping with the weight of luggage I was riding with, over roads and dirt tracks, gravel and unmade roads with confidence and assurance.

Crash bars – a useful platform for cameras. A footrest alternative. An anchor point for tent ropes and on one occasion they did exactly what they were actually designed to do.

LED spotlights – provided illumination in the dark, unsurprisingly, but their main purpose was to provide additional reasons for drivers in busy urban areas to notice this lost traveller as I navigated through foreign places while trying to understand local signs (or lack thereof). One spotlight still clings on with gaffer tape and cable ties after impact with tarmac and tram track in Russia.

Cable ties and gaffer tape – held anything and everything together when the original fixing failed through neglect or accident, including the right side mirror, which suffered from 'droop' but held on all the way after the same tram track incident in Irkutsk.

Additional fuel cans – were a great idea for the couple of times I needed them. They provided a comforting insurance where fuel was sparse. On two occasions, getting me to the next available fuel stop. A bit of forward planning on my part would have meant they never got used, in which case they would have been a waste of time, but they weren't so they were worthwhile having.

Camping gear – when a tent becomes your home it's worth having the right one. I bought the biggest tent that I could find that packed up the smallest. By the end it had a few tears and rips. The stitching was failing around the zip. But it did the job. It kept the rain out several times, the masses of mosquitoes out in the Siberian forests and separated me from what I suspect was a bear in the middle of the night on one occasion. I couldn't ask much more from a few sheets of sewn nylon. I left it in a charity shop in Apollo Bay on the Great Ocean Road.

Three-season sleeping bag – warm enough when it was cold and a comfy mattress when it wasn't.

UVA sunshade tarp – I made copious use of a one-metre-square sunshade with one pole and a couple of guy ropes in various configurations. As a porch extension to the tent, or as a sunshade on front of the bike, the possibilities were endless!

Riding gear – an RST Pro Series textile jacket and IXS trousers with removable lining and plenty of air vents meant I could cope with sub-zero temperatures over the Alps and the extreme heat of the Australian outback in mid-summer. My riding gear was a perfect combination of comfort, practicality and protection.

Shark flip-front helmet – a fantastic aid to communication. It was a cool, stylish open-face lid when cruising through towns and warm countryside, and a great protection from the elements and suicidal insects at speed.

Wulfsport trial boots – gave me the flexibility to be able to walk when needed and the confidence of a protective motorcycle boot when asked.

Gloves – two pairs of lightweight summer gloves saw me through hotter climes. A ventilated pair of leather gloves cried enough by the time I got to Australia but a replacement pair of Dri-Rider ventilated textile gloves purchased from a Darwin motorcycle dealer did a great job for the hot regions. A pair of expensive Halvarssons all-weather gloves provided enough warmth in association with the heated grips to deal with colder climes.

Android phone – The 'all-in-one' adventure rider's tech tool – GPS mapping via the maps.me app, email, phone, book reader, camera, video camera, translator, blog-writing tool, online hotel and flights booking, currency converter and online banking, all from one device, charged from a twelve volt connector on the bike. It was invaluable.

Guesses at distances and dates – guesses at arrival times at borders for visa applications worked out about right. I waited in Georgia for my Azerbaijani visa to start, but arrived at Kazak and Russian borders as visas were due to start and I didn't have to race to exit borders before they expired.

Tyres – a pair of Heidenau K73 tyres were fitted prior to departure. The rear was replaced early in Turkey by a Continental TKC80, which provided all the confidence I needed on the rough roads and dirt tracks of Kazakhstan. The front Heidenau lasted all the way to Vladivostok over snowy mountains, hot summer roads, gravel and dirt tracks, fields and melted tarmac, finally arriving in Vladivostok in a deluge of rain after covering 13,000 miles. The replacement Pirelli MT60 lasted a lap of Australia. A MITAS enduro rear fitted in Darwin, I fully expect to last until the end of time!

Money – my budget proved sound to the end. Carrying $2500USD in cash saw me across Azerbaijan, Kazakhstan and Russia, exchanging the last few 'bucks' in South Korea. A credit card took up the slack for shipping costs and air tickets. While I didn't live extravagantly, there was room for a couple of comparatively luxurious accommodations along the way.

Books – twenty-eight books swapped or purchased from second-hand bookshops or downloaded to my phone or tablet, ranging from autobiographies to science fiction and fantasy novels, provided the literary inspiration and escape into worlds beyond our own on starry nights reading by torchlight away from civilization, surrounded by the natural world.

Me! – I didn't break or fail. Apart from a few bruises to limbs and ego, nothing was damaged. My anticoagulation was simply not an issue. My mechanical heart valve merrily ticked away. My INR remained manageable throughout, despite the scenes of unimaginable horror painted by the nurse in the anti-coag clinic before I left.

What didn't work or failed – electrical gadgets suffered the worst:

iPod – my trusty old 'wheel' iPod died of LCD failure. A cheap MP3 player replacement survived until the last days of travel before giving up on providing any usable volume.

MUVI action cam – failed early into the journey after the charging socket detached from the circuit board while in Italy.

Power bank – one charger was a victim of the same issue as the charging socket failing. A replacement survived the journey.

Android tablet (x2) – taken as a means to read without carrying numerous paper books. The first one suffered the same charging port failure. A cheap replacement died with a cracked screen.

HP notebook laptop – survived intact and was used to edit YouTube videos until the sound card failed. It is still serviceable and still being used, albeit silently.

Charging cables – for phone and tablets. I've lost count of how many; they are fragile little things that don't take much abuse.

Airbed – failed early on, but Mother Nature provided a comfortable sleeping bed once I got used to her curves and bumps.

Wood burning stove – junked after realising that a pile of sticks and logs on a fire will do the same job without the need for any equipment other than what the natural world provides.

Non-sterling charges – a cost I don't want to think about. I haven't worked out how much I've paid on non-sterling transaction fees for debit or credit card purchases or cash withdrawals.

Australian quarantine – enough said at the time. Suffice to say highway robbery is not as lucrative.

English language – my spelling and grammar let me down frequently. They still do writing this. But getting the story across is sometimes more important than correcting my own basic English failings.

Like all the best stories, life goes on. I don't know where mine is going to go or how it's going to end, but there are more chapters to be written yet. Do you ever find yourself staring at an aeroplane high in the sky and wondering where it's heading? I'm doing it a lot. Excluding flight distances (approximately 13,650 miles), I covered a total of 25,454 road miles.

The things that spring to mind right now about the memorable bits include crossing the Alps, a month in Italy and the Tuscan hills under fabulous star-filled night skies. Greek beaches, a week exploring Tbilisi and crossing the Caspian Sea by cargo vessel. The arrival in Khabarovsk after riding the Trans-Siberian Highway. The intense heat of the Australian outback and the Great Ocean Road. All of New Zealand! The Grand Canyon and Route 66. There are lots more that will keep me dreaming of further adventures for many years to come.

I hope my musings have been entertaining, informative and even amusing at times. I've tried to write in a way that I hope has provided some insight into my thoughts and experiences during this adventure, in a fashion that illustrated the reality of living on the road for a year of my life. I don't know where the next chapter starts. I hope I can add more as time reveals its plans to me. But, for now, thank you for getting this far with me. 'Moving on'…

Ciao for now
Mark

'RESTLESS' **– Blackberry Smoke**

20 FINAL WORD

The beauty of travelling around the world is that it allows you to get altitude. No, I don't mean airplane altitude. I mean it allows you to get a big-picture perspective on things, to see the various ways cultures mesh and collide with one another and how the different streams of history have eroded and hardened each country's social structures into their respective places.

You realise that much of what you believed to be unique in your home country is often universal, and that much of what you thought was universal is often specific to your home country.

You realise that humans are by and large the same, with the same needs, the same desires and the same awful biases that pit them haplessly against each other.

You realise that, no matter how much you see or how much you learn about the world, there's always more — that with every new destination discovered, you become aware of a dozen others, and with every new piece of knowledge obtained you only become more aware of how much you really don't know.

You realise that you will never be able to explore or encounter all of these destinations because you realise that the more you spread the breadth of your experience across the globe, the thinner and more meaningless it becomes.

You realise that there's something to be said for limiting oneself, not just geographically but also emotionally. That there's a certain depth of experience and meaning that can only be achieved when one picks a single piece of creation and says, "This is it. This is where I belong."

Perpetual world travel literally gives you a whole world of experience. But it also takes another away.